Prison notes.

Let's be free humans.

PRISON NOTES

First edition. August 13, 2023.

ISBN: 979-8215168561

Written by Juan Manuel Ramírez Magallón.

Table of Contents

By JUAN MANUEL RAMIREZ MAGALLON

Dedication:
To my little children, to my Masonic brothers,
Friends and fellow fighters,
nephews, my wife, my mother and relatives.

JUAN MANUEL RAMÍREZ MAGALLÓN

First edition

Magallon, Juan M.
Diary of a prisoner / Juan Manuel Ramirez Magallón
Mexico. 2023

Introduction.

The national security problem is alarming and in the state of Michoacán crime prevails: kidnapping, rape, corruption, the collection of property, disappearance of people and the collection or extortion for having, doing, selling and even deserving. In the last ten years, the cartels have increased the effects on society and strengthened their relationship with high government officials, for which reason they are practically considered the second government, they interfere in matters of law such as: agrarian, criminal, civil, commercial and family; at territorial levels, such as: ejidal, communal, municipal, state, national and international; they influence the activities: educational, religious, health, economic, agricultural production, livestock, mining and fishing; its influence is so powerful that music and cinema make production dedicated to drug trafficking, affecting the free and healthy development of children and youth, altering the tranquility and mental health of society.

When the family is harmed, it is when even the most cowardly fights, crime touched the interests of innocent families, which is why an armed movement is made in Michoacan society, called community police, in our case as an indigenous community we arm the police or community guard and self-defense groups to safeguard the fundamental rights of our town and our community, such as freedom, peace, order, respect, dignity, etc.

This work is written from prison by one of the members of the Aquila self-defense group, which is why it talks about life in prison and the prisoners themselves; the work is suitable for an audience over 14 years of age, in the case of a minor an adult is required to avoid negative hermeneutics, in the next chapters we talk about life in a federal maximum security prison, where the body and the mind are much more hurt, but in the common law the person is much more denigrated. We will try not to write a book with vulgar language, our intention is to settle the life of a prisoner in federal prison, the sensations, feelings, sufferings and frustrations; We find the rejection of other points of view of life by prisoners who have a high degree of danger and their comparison with prisoners who claim to be innocent.

This work mentions how the community police, through investigation and testimony of the people, discovers or shares information regarding organized crime, its links with the government, the affiliation of authorities with these villains, we describe the damage that exists in the country and the activities against society by organized crime.

The work presented is descriptive of social problems caused by organized crime and even by the government itself, or rather, by government elements at all levels.

From prison, from a dreamer, to other prisoners who can go wherever they want.

Day 6 in prison.

On the sixth day of prison, I start with a draft of the prison notes, with the intention of one day sharing them with the public. I will start by talking about the emergence of the self-defense group, but not before telling them that a few days ago I was arrested at forty-one five detainees, 39 are direct companions and 5 were our prisoners for working as hawks and hit men, after our arrest they have taken us to the SEIDO where the constitutional term has elapsed and they have made us available to the second judge of Jalapa Veracruz, so Therefore, they transferred us to perote, a cold prison in the mountains; preventive detention was agreed due to the seriousness of the alleged crimes, for which we will remain in prison in this prison; they transfer us from the separator building to the population; distributed to various modules, where we will remain for many years if it is our bad luck. Someone gave me a notebook and a tube of pen ink, in the cell from where I will write what I see and experience every day, at least when there is strength.

It is the winter of 2011 and crime is highly organized, but above all active in the looting of fine woods, such as mahogany and blackwood, they steal fuel extracting it from the trailers of the carriers to feed the short trucks that take the iron boleo to Manzanillo, this practice consists of lifting the iron stones that rest on the surface. Nobody says or does anything because life would be in the middle, the communal and ejido authorities only limit themselves to signing permits and keeping silent.

In that community of San Miguel, it is represented by a president of the commissioner who has a notion of good community management. Its mottos are "everyone united and everything belongs to everyone", "no one rich, no one poor", "the greatest interest is the common one and it is above all things". In the winter of 2011, this president of the commissioner moved to the neighboring city and talked with his first cousin, a law student and a graduate in philosophy, whom he hired to work with him on his project, of course he was going to accept, he resigned from his job and after a few days it was made available to the community.

He arrived at the town when the precious clouds loaded with water were shining in the sky, waiting for the moment to vent their fury, in that territory the stones are worth a lot and the capitalists already have a presence, the enormous craters are present a short distance from the town, the people He has already eaten the delicacy of the capital. Meanwhile, a string of trailers removes thousands of tons of iron ore leaving nothing but contamination and discord, true, they generate jobs, but not for the indigenous people but for outsiders.

The capices and the white naguas.

That community carries great vices and defects, discord and struggle, greed and generosity, in previous decades interests arise, and the community is divided by "the white naguas" and "the capices" (pseudonym relative to the poet, philosopher and lawyer Efrén Capiz Villegas, founder of the UCEZ), "the white naguas" are skillful negotiators, their relationship transcends rubbing shoulders with the priest, with crime, with the municipal president and with the companies that loot the community, they criminally agree on the amounts money, with which they will silence "the Indians", they give them a million and a half, which has to be distributed among 479 community members, while the same amount is distributed between Luis González (mining boss) and "the blacks" or "the white naguas".

A rivalry arises that costs the life of the leader of "the capices" of the coastal region, since his ideals are opposed to capitalist interests, in the 80's that leader channels his strength to close the mining company for five years , with his group he tried to obtain the concession and exploitation for his community, but his ideals and ambitions took his life, one night on April 29, he was assassinated by the secretary of the commissioner, this seduced by the payment of 70 million that The miner sent him to 5 cowards who, with premeditation, said that the judiciary was going to make rounds and the minor judge went to tell the capices to put away their weapons and they went out to dinner, when they were having dinner they spoke to the leader so that he would sign some documents and they seized him unarmed, he lifted up his shirt and said that he had no weapon, that they would give him a chance, but his enemies were very afraid of him, that is why a group of four was formed to assassinate him. For decades "the white naguas" distributed the amount of 250 pesos to each Indian annually, or they paid them with drunkenness in the town festivals, later, in 2006 they gave them a little more, 1500 pesos per year as a result of the pressure exerted by Carlos Ramos with the community, until 2012 when the royalties for the exploitation of iron from the Los Tenamaxtles mine were obtained, a fight led by the community property commissioner named Agustín Villanueva Ramirez. Obtaining 100 million pesos distributed among the community members and a month-to-month royalty deposit for each of those registered, is when organized crime increases the fee to the community and charges 750,000 pesos per month for extortion or collection of floor. It should be noted that the community already paid a fee of 100,000 pesos per month since 2007, a fee derived from a transportation company made up of community members and the product of a government and mining trust. On December 27, 2011, the community decided to block the bypass of the town to obtain royalties for the extraction of iron, high-grade mineral (90% grade) and the second iron reserve in Mexico, a magnificent place, full of huge trees, hills full of dry forests, abundant water and wealth everywhere, however, there is marginalization and extreme poverty.

It is June 3, 2013 in that town everything seems ordinary and nothing out of the ordinary, a Ford 150 pickup truck, double cab, white, comes through the muddy streets of the town, it runs slowly avoiding the potholes and ill-made and irregular bumps of the town; People greet him because he is the president of the community's community property commissioner. It is a morning in which the formation of the communal guard group is managed and after this it will not be possible for things to be the same. 6 people meet and decide to arm themselves against organized crime.

That June 3, 2013, the self-defense group was formed, made up of a handful of men, six people willing to die, that day they were visited by a federal police agent who went to invite them to form an opposition group to the cartel. They met with weapons of various calibers, mostly 12, 16, 20 gauge shotguns, .22 rifles, M1, R15, Ak 47 and pistols. Its members were mostly children of community members and community members of the indigenous community, they lasted in a camp for approximately a month, until reaching a number of 100 community guard assets. Then they took over the town, the municipal seat, on July 24, 2013, detaining 7 municipal police officers for a few hours and confiscating two pistols and two R15s, few weapons to deal with the bad guys, don't you think? The navy had already gone to secure the weapons of the municipal police due to the risk of an invasion of the town by the self-defense groups, so they lasted with the domain and control of the town for 20 days. On August 13, they were disarmed by the federal and state governments, they are taken to SEIDO and later to federal prison number five.

The detained writer is shocked to find himself in the dark world of punishment dens, where diabolical, profane, stupid, sick, popular beliefs and naive religious beliefs move. The creeds are multiple and in different deities, there are those who believe in death as a god and they dedicate their faith to it, I think that is why in some parts of the country, along the road, you can find altars to "the holy death", the same one that "favors" criminals, because all the deaths that criminals commit are dedicated to it, many deaths are worse than sacrificing a small animal, they begin with torture, while the person is tied up they cut, drown, mutilate, extractions, bruises and electric shocks, this in order to obtain required and useful information for the criminal, is not only a criminal practice, it is a government practice. Criminals are addicted to stupid things like superstitions, drugs, gossip, superfluous things like vanities and luxuries. The ideal world of criminals is the one we live in, in this world there is a large mass of population that is submissive and addicted, a corrupt government and a high degree of criminal activity, we are talking about an economic paradise. But where would it take us to be all criminals? To the destruction of society, to chaos.

In prison and in society we find a zoo, a circus that teaches us to act and live, as a clear example we find prisons, in these almost all are nicknamed after animals and in society they are called ox, however, on television we find politicians doing tricks and doing grace in order to get the vote; We also find prostitutes invested with greatness, criminals who govern our country, hiding that pig they bring behind them, no one comes to power without violating the rights of others in a system where democracy is a distortion and synonymous with dictatorship.

In the psychopathic life of the prisons, those who have diseases such as syndrome, various mental illnesses appear, these pathologies are not only found in the inmates but also in the security and administrative personnel of the social reintegration centers; These characters play a certain dynamic, a role that they have to play or rather the role assigned to them by society and the system. According to the codification of the person, it is the self or role that he plays in society and prisons are a clear example of society. The problem is of reason, it is in this faculty where the problem lies, criminals believe they are right when they deprive another of life or property, however, it is a disease that distorts reason to irrationality, the problem is a pathology, mental vices that do not allow the criminal to develop virtue. A criminal expressed his needs and said: "I dress, fit, eat, drink, have fun, I like good things, bring money and society has to pay for that, leaving prison I will continue committing crimes", is this the degree of cynicism in criminals. Another prisoner said that this type of criminal should be killed, since they represent nothing more than a high-impact crime. They have the audacity to say that they don't like to work and presume that they can get everything by committing crimes.

Criminals sleep like kings during the day and commit crimes at night, or vice versa, they avoid sleeping sober at night because nightmares torture them, they are ridden by the dead, the dead, the child, the dismembered, the raped, the snake, the dead man's head, the flying hand that wants to hang them, the dogs, the police, the army and many nocturnal projections that stalk them if they sleep at night. This reveals how damaged their brains are, manifesting enormous traumas, some due to the lack of a father or mother, domestic violence, an abused childhood, rape, etc. Others were traumatized by their economic situation or lack, hunger awakened their animal instincts and led them to survive by snatching the belongings of others, killing, kidnapping, destroying the lives of others. It is extreme selfishness, a real problem in society. It is necessary to eradicate this type of behavior as far as possible, in society they are badly characterized by wolves and sheep, this is extreme. Society is stalked by agents that devour humans, and we live in a perfect system in which the conditions for crime exist.

The true belief of criminals is not defined or found because they are changeable, disloyal, fickle, wandering, heretics and weak in their creeds, now they may be believing in holy death, after a while they are believing in Christ, praying as true converts but In reality it is a farce, an escape valve for mental pressure, a theater, a deception to society to continue committing crimes or to oneself and to be able to tell the mind that one is good and be able to rest one's conscience. The criminal does not cease to be by going to leave the burden of conscience to a god, this is achieved when the damage is fully repaired and the damage is healed throughout life. When his instinct needs the recipe again, he resorts to it and commits a crime to obtain the satisfaction of his needs. The criminal applies all his ability to commit a crime. There are other degrees of criminality, in which pleasure is acquired by committing a crime, such is the case of serial killers, who do not seek to profit from their crime, but commit crimes in order to satisfy their criminal instinct and obtain pleasure in their actions.

In prison they circulate or traffic in pills, narcotics and psychotropics to be able to face themselves, since reality presents itself to us humans in a crude way, it slaps us in the face at all times and criminals do not like slaps from Consciousness, they support being treated like dogs by those of higher rank, but they do not even allow themselves to be treated reproachfully, that is why they block themselves with drugs. Some delinquents confessed that their superiors whipped them, hit them with rulers, rods, slaps, insults, kicks, etc. They love that because then the boss consoles them with drugs, which is deducted from the payment, ending the day of the raya, giving life to the raya store, similar to Porfirio Díaz ("the crybaby") where the landowners They were stealing labor from the worker and peasant, discounting or paying in kind. Thus, the problem in society worsens when there are children and wives of criminals in the streets, these little ones follow the example of crime. It is a disgrace to have a father or mother who is so weak that the only thing he knows how to do very well is commit crimes, no matter how professional they are.

Society feeds criminal behavior, since there is no surveillance of family members and they do not file complaints when the offender commits criminal behavior; families should take care of the behavior of other families and themselves, criminals should not be protected. The correction must be immediate and timely, starting in childhood, correcting incorrect behaviors and not reproducing behaviors that hurt childhood. It should be channeled according to the profile of the youth to carry out activities according to their profile, young people with characteristics or profiles vulnerable to illegal conduct can be channeled to professions where skill, strength, hard work and military disciplines are dealt with. Here in prison the guards are potential criminals, they lower themselves to improper treatment and behavior, most of the prison workers do not have humanitarian principles, they justify themselves in a certain way because the inmates act like caged animals, it is not correct to generalize in the behavior of the inmates and in the guards, there are those who remain upright and are not contaminated by criminal wickedness.

Disarmament of the self-defense group.

On August 14, the people of Aquila were covered in terror when they perceived the arrival of criminals dressed as soldiers and ministerial officers, they entered the homes from where they extracted weapons of all calibers, money, jewelry, and valuables; some homes belonged to criminals, in that event they went for the leaders of the self-defense groups and community guards, these groups carried 12, 16, 20 caliber shotguns, .22 rifles and some R15 and other calibers, in this act of disarmament they were present More than 1,000 elements of various police forces, including the Mexican army that acted in favor of the Mexican cartels and at that point in Michoacán were the Knights Templar, a criminal group that began in opposition to "Los Zetas" and derives from the faction from the Michoacan family.

In the disarmament they did not refuse to hand over their weapons, some of high caliber were confiscated from criminals and police. Well, we know that organized crime and the political structure of the municipality, the state and the country work together. One of the comments with the greatest impact on the life of the narrator has been in which they point out that the interim governor is a political relative of one of the heads of the dominant criminal group in the state, "our soldiers are all good Mexicans who, with their resistance organized, we are opposed to a destiny in which one lives only to serve a master, we are opposed to those criminals who only reflect cowardice and lack of heart, however the baseness in values and ethics in the instances scares us, that lack of morality that characterizes them, we are scared by the cruelty with which the ministerial police and the army operate, it denigrates us to know that commanders of the men to whom we pay our taxes, are co-authors of organized crime, today it is said that Mexico belongs to criminals and it seems so, they see the people as objects, as cattle, as labor, the government agencies defend the interests of these groups and it does not hurt them to leave children without a father, they cannot destroy families, engendering terror in our homes or dishonoring our nation, vegetating behind the uniform of public servants, it is outrageous to know that corrupt elements raise people up and make them disappear.

Today we live in the hope of getting out of this maximum security prison, in which many politicians and public servants should be, criminals who have us here. We know that not all Mexicans are the same and it is for the good that it is worth fighting for and the effort to make a Mexico where the good have a place free of crime is dedicated to them. Not all public servants are the same, there are those who have humanitarian ideals and values, they are the ones who work giving their best, however, the tendency to carry out undesirable behaviors and against the country prevails. The idea that all Mexicans are equal predominates. The commitment of good people is to transmit the ideals to their children, those humanitarian goals out of love for humanity. Let's educate our children for good.

Our cartridges are legal because we buy them with our money in armories authorized by the government, invoiced and many of the weapons we brought are registered, we are referring to 12, 16 and 20 shotguns, 22 rifles and other calibers that are not exclusive to the army, We confiscated the weapons from a corporal and some hit men who stopped and from a searched house of a criminal nicknamed "palillo", an AK 47 is from the family of caciques, that is how we have been providing security to the town since the 24th of July to August 14, the day we were detained and disarmed by the army and the ministerial police, who brought four informers from the same community, the pretext of executing the arrest warrants is pure ministerial stuff, the order came out of interim governor who sent the secretary of the government of Michoacán one Saturday to come to an agreement with hitmen, drug shooters, criminal co-perpetrators, widows of hitmen, money launderers and supporters of the cartel. The municipal president teamed up with the criminal group and with traitors from the indigenous communities that make up the municipality, they fight to stay in power and continue providing criminal security services in exchange for the monthly fee. Added to these is the trustee, who hides criminals in his ranch, just like the chiefs of the municipality who hide armed criminals inside their properties. We do not rule out the participation of the municipal president of the PRI in the coup against the communal guard and self-defense group who makes statements to the contrary and false accusations, being that in a communal guard filter his life was spared for being the first degree uncle of 9 elements of the community police.

This character is considered a traitor to his ideals in which he was formed alongside the leader José Ramirez Verduzco, who lost his life in 1989, dejected for maintaining his firmness in his ideals. Among his priorities were the defense of land, natural resources and the rights of indigenous peoples, this leader is recognized for the drive to obtain the presidential resolution where they are endowed with communal land. The PRI president is a henchman of a social fighter who repented of his ideals and entered the evangelical religion to hide his evil and disguise himself as a good person, after dragging excesses of alcohol, marijuana, prostitutes and other worldly vices in his past. The curious thing is that his family does not follow him in his religious conversion because they do not believe such a change. When the self-defense group emerges, this partisan leader flees to the state of Nayarit and his family remains within the perimeter of the territory taken over by the communal self-defense group.

The group of pro-organized crime is made up of former presidents and community officials and the city council, they take refuge in the neighboring state, where the governor grants them a roof, pantries and coverage to the media, in which they point out that they were expelled from the community and the municipality, this being false, they displaced themselves, that is, they abandoned the criminal plaza, at no time were they told anything, they acted because of their complicity with organized crime and cried before they were beaten, these advised by evil, they began his informative attack through radio and newspapers, television and electronic media.

They organized narco marches in which, alongside the criminals, they paraded asking for "peace for the people" "not the community police", they were defamed and pretended to be victims when in reality they are the perpetrators and thieves, as proof there is the participation of the dismissed commissioned in the granting of permits for the extraction of iron bole from the communal surface of the property called "La Estanzuela", this subject named Villanueva E. has no scruples, denounced that the self-defense groups had broken into his house and that among forty they had raped His daughter, being that such a girl was pregnant by one of his chalanes and to hide her dishonorable deed, told her father that she had been raped. This guy left the community, leaving his ranch, taking his cows to a borrowed ranch. In previous dates, he had cut down a few hectares of thick trees and destroyed that vegetation to plant cornfields and pastures, changing the use of the soil. It is also a crime to give communal permission to extract iron without the authorization of the assembly, as the commissioner did, by authorizing the plaza chief to extract iron.

The criminals made a mix by combining political and religious life, the presidency united with the transnational company and all coordinated with the cartel, they barred all expression from the people and the community by controlling all expressions of authority and representation at the service of the organized crime. Thus, we find community groups colluding with the cartel and with the interim governor, who is said to be related to the top leader of the cartel, a certain professor. All this social, economic, business, political, religious and community structure against the self-defense group, thus we discover that the cartel influences all the expressions of a people, when it becomes as entrenched as the Templarios cartel was.

The ideals of self-defense are secular, without partisan or political tendencies nor does it distinguish races, it is the fight for the security of our people and for the freedom to decide who governs us and demand transparency from the government. Our fight is for peace, for freedom, for justice, our fight is not to be condemned to live as foreigners in our own land, our fight for the social, political, economic dignity of our state. That is why several communiqués were published in the electronic media and in newspapers. We do not seek power for power's sake, much less introduce another cartel.

In the town there are offended, we believe that they are the ones who were harmed by organized crime when their sons, husbands, daughters or a relative were killed, regardless of whether they were economically, morally or legally affected; We have evidence and it is a matter of looking for each offended party and the legal evidence that remains, this is how they leave a people hurt by the actions of the scourges. All individuals who have acted illegally against their family get used to doing the same with society and they reproduce this pattern as a form of modus vivendi, they join criminal triads to obtain better results. Criminal systems are defended by social sectors, which, in a certain way, benefit from illegal activities, since these groups occupy third parties to launder their money, invest and ensure their permanence in crime. This is how they control communities, ejidos, companies, institutions and wealthy people, resulting in a criminal arena.

When the ministerial officers went to disarm the self-defense group, they entered various houses, offices and properties of the affected indigenous community without search warrants, in the same way they stole everything in their path, the army shot women in the feet, among them they, pregnant, generating terror, my mother carrying my young daughter and my wife four months pregnant made them cross the river with bullets.

Without a commission document or search or arrest warrant, more than a thousand elements went to violate the communities; In the case of indigenous communities, property should be respected and the introduction of armed elements into their territory should be ordered by a competent Judge, since it is considered that the community members are the owners of these lands and anyone who wants to enter within its perimeter should ask its inhabitants for permission through its communal and legal commission. In that famous disarmament, the ministerials and the army let go of the detainees' wallets and took their money and then returned their wallets without cash, they took away their weapons and valuables, such as: chains, cell phones, rings , money, luxury weapons, etc.

In that disarmament, they tied their hands and feet with belts and some with handcuffs, they threw them like pigs into the trucks, one on top of the other, those white trucks without license plates ran at full speed along the coastal highway until they reached Lázaro Cárdenas, where they went up all the detainees to a truck. With humiliations, insults and threats they kicked them during the journey, they put their feet on their backs, the barrels of the rifles rested on the soft flesh of the detainees. They took photos of them and uploaded them to the media and social networks, generating insult and damage to honor. On that occasion of the disarmament, the community police officers brought with them five hit men and hawks from a neighboring municipality as prisoners, who posed as community members so that they would not release them, since those of their cartel already wanted them to assassinate them because those of the community police made them talk.

When the forty community police officers were detained, they detained another ten compañeros and released them in the town where the leader of the criminals operated, they did this with the intention of having them assassinated. Meanwhile, they scared the community members they were carrying in the white vans with threats to hand them over to the plaza chief, they were handcuffed like little iguanas, with their hands behind their backs, and they took them on the beds of the vans at full speed, the coastal highway of Michoacán is pure curve and abundant in potholes and bumps, because these trucks did not stop they passed very hard, leaving serious consequences in the detainees, their bodies crushed by so much metal blows. Ministerial police are insensitive, they are just like criminals, they can violate the fundamental rights of people, cause them damage and injuries without remorse, this due to a lack of ethics and professional preparation.

Made available to the poster.

Transferred to the SEIDO accused of organized crime, carrying weapons exclusive to the army with the possibility of spending many years behind federal bars is what leaves them with the intention of freeing their people from a cartel. The ministerials made the informative part in front of some detainees and in the same way distributed weapons to everyone, those who were caught unarmed were accused of collecting weapons and cartridges. They said "here they fuck, there are weapons for everyone and there are even plenty", it was true they had disarmed more than 200 members of the community and they only brought 40 plus 5 hit men, that is, there were plenty of weapons. The head of the operation asked "what weapon did you have? They didn't even know that, and the community members incriminated themselves by pointing out the weapon they brought, those who denied bringing a weapon, because there were those who did not bring it, charged them with the crime of stockpiling, such was my case.

After all, the hitmen take out the caste, they threaten to say that they had kidnapped them if the self-defense groups do not say that they are part of the self-defense group; The chief of operations asks them for the names of the streets, where the community police officers were detained, they didn't even know that, some are detained up to 500 meters away from the point indicated in the informative report, he asked us to tell him the names and points where They were arrested, being a flawed police report and full of errors. Among the crimes of illegal search and abuse of authority found in the informative part is where it indicates the community auditorium as a "municipal" auditorium, it indicates having detained the leaders in these places and it was not true, the community leader named Agustín Villanueva Ramirez They detained him at his home approximately 30 kilometers away, at the "La Naranja" ranch and transported by helicopter.

They set up a false scenario, in which they point out that there is a stockpiling of weapons, this being a false saying, where suddenly, for not doing the job correctly, they gathered weapons when they were disarming people and they stole their luxury weapons Assault shotguns, sawed-off weapons, vintage pistols, and rifles with accessories never appeared in the report, much less fragmentation grenades and high-caliber sawed-off weapons that I have in my weapons record as general secretary of the group. They pointed out what they wanted, so an unknown park appeared, for example: a single 50-caliber shot, without preserving the purity of the evidence, the ministerial officers made lots of weapons and parks to incriminate the elements of the community police , they maneuvered the weapons in such a way that the chain of custody was broken and to indicate precision they point to arrest coordinates, this being false, however the objective was achieved, it was to dismantle the self-defense group that was about to explode in all corners of the municipality.

International organizations are far from human rights, they are only subject to issuing recommendations and they are not enough for so many violations of human rights worldwide, in addition, the governments of nations are disloyal and liars, they hide nature at will. of the facts, giving negative reports to the human rights complaints made by the governed, here the government defends the attacks against the community, being an act with possible reparation for damages.

The government went through the streets disarming at will and detaining the leaders of the community and the self-defense group, the workers of transportation and mining companies, they took them out of their vehicles and arrested them, putting weapons and cartridges on them, this was not It was merely an act of the agents, but there was someone who pointed to the sympathizers of the community leader and incriminated them for signaling. This is how they incriminated people who were at home, at work, in their vehicles and those who were walking down the street.

This is how an illegal arrest of the self-defense group "for a free Aquila" takes place, and on August 14, 2013, an equivalent of 200 people were disarmed by an operation of 1,000 elements and only 40 community police officers were prosecuted. The processed elements were taken to the SEIDO and later to the federal prison in Perote Veracruz; the government makes this distancing to hinder the process and avoid the speed of the process, they send the detainees away with the intention that their relatives and those who lead their defense are unable to make the promotions quickly and this delays the process. In the detention, the status of the detainees is not considered, for example, if they belong to an ethnic group or indigenous community, if they are workers, peasants or of some specific social status, they only focus on affecting the person and generate their entanglement in the country's penal system, which works like a spider's web, traps, but is difficult to disentangle.

The system treats people who rebel against the system worse than criminals, it is the case of these unfortunate self-defense groups who were deprived of their liberty, a major crime is being poor, not having money to offer an adequate defense, in the one that enforces their rights and guarantees a fair and transparent process, with equal opposition. When the poor are left at a disadvantage because you do not offer an adequate defense, they are left defenseless and the injustice is repeated, but now directly exercised by the state. The legal uncertainty is carried out by the public ministry and takes advantage of it because the experience in the violation of human rights is a repetitive practice and in bad faith, they repeat this behavior throughout the activities of administration of 'justice'.

The authority does not have enough tact, nor does it care to protect people's rights, once designated as criminals they go viciously and do not miss the opportunity to vent their anger against whoever is criminal or innocent, this action is often used by the defense and turns it into a reason to obtain the freedom of the defendant, since international treaties regarding human rights condemn torture and harassment in detention. A point that is not lacking is the robbery of the captors, they do not miss the opportunity to loot, avoiding all evidence, they do not allow recordings or photography to avoid being exhibited as thieves and starving.

The self-defense group was supported by some councilors, who joined the self-defense groups to face the violence generated by the cartel in power, such was the case of the municipalities of Chinicuila, Coalcomán, Aguililla, La Ruana and others. . We consider these councilors as rulers who responsibly listen to the needs of their population and join the interests of the people. In the case of Aquila, the communal guard suffered the attack of the municipal presidency as the mayor was in collusion with the criminals and made a front against the self-defense when entering on August 20, 2013 with the army and ministerials, murdering two indigenous community members and beating the community on their own land, it appears to be a triumphant entrance to the municipal palace, this within the communal perimeter. Generating the return of crime to the population. Making it clear that the interests of the local government are above popular interests and sealing their affiliation to the combat group. Even if they arrest the entire town, the need for security remains in force and the petitioner will not give up until the need is met. Therefore, bars do not kill the truth or the need of the population. However, they are not the only or the last political prisoners for social struggles, this comforts me and warms me in the cold cell that I find myself in.

In group detentions, they harass them to the point of taking their minds to a state that is not capable of detecting human rights violations, keeping them hungry, giving them few liquids, bothering them at all times with questions and the despotic and arrogant attitude of the agents are present at all times, they talk to them to ask information about their private life, without the assistance of a defense attorney and because they are the judging, violating and arresting authority, complaints due to lack of evidence do not proceed. The authority is the first to violate individual guarantees and encourage violence, the government's interest is to defend and guarantee big capital, the population is a third party to harm at the pleasure of the oppressor and the businessman; When the government stops fulfilling its functions and commits acts that violate the rights of the population, it becomes organized crime. I have no nominative to name the authority in the case of colluding with organized crime, such is the case of the interim governor of Michoacan right now.

In the university of the immoral and illegal, ways of committing a crime are learned, from the most common of the criminal scum to the most sophisticated of the undesirable behavioral ways of existing and acting; In this university, the internships are carried out right here, there are those who make their bodies a drug store, a cover for radio communication devices, they use their skin as a blackboard, the drugs are swallowed with plastic to be able to pass the checkpoints and control of review centers. As well as, the drug is put into the organ of defecation or through the vagina in the case of women, calling it "trunk", "panochazo", just like an object. Once they are free from the surveillance of the jailers, they vomit to obtain the drug or extract it from their private parts.

This behavior is often not at the free will of the transporter, they are forced by the inmates themselves, others find it necessary to act in this illegal manner due to the economic needs they experience and see the possibility of doing business with this dangerous practice. and demeaning. How many cases are there where the husband is imprisoned and the wife is later discovered transporting drugs inside the prisons, leaving their children helpless, who follow the path of their parents, making an insecure society. It should be noted that, inside a federal prison, a gram of drugs can cost thousands of pesos, a digital device can cost up to one hundred thousand pesos, which are deposited and transported in the anus, in the same way that inmates keep them. in the butt Not only family members do illegal business inside the prisons, the biggest business is for the directors, operational heads, custodians and for employees of the prisons. Only those who have enough money can maintain the luxuries inside the prison, they can sell call services, extort from the prison, run their cartel or cells from inside the prisons. The reviews inside the prisons have the function of promoting business, confiscating drugs and communication devices so that new ones can be acquired.

Criminals are evil, envious and they dedicate themselves to screwing anyone, therefore, they reveal who has an advantage over them and make them fall into disgrace, this feature has not been used by the government. A criminal is characterized by jealousy, distrust and envy, he cannot see that another surpasses him, that leads him to try to disgrace the other, even if misfortune later kills him. The criminal will seek to decompose the existence of others. That is why the little shops inside the prisons do not last, they are thundered, in addition, these little shops have a cost of parking, the prisons charge for this practice and operating outside the prison's permits has serious consequences.

Thus, the drug and device trafficker inside a prison has a cartel that supports him and a corrupt system that allows him in exchange for payment. No matter the degree of appointment, honor, or type of instance, they all have a cost and a degree of participation. All social circles are vulnerable to the temptations of easy money, to forced decisions. In prison the virtues are denoted, but they are nothing compared to the vices and baseness, good people become bad when they do not have their defined ideals, weakness allows them to acquire criminal attitudes. Good people maintain their lucidity and human principles about the temptations that arise daily in a center of acquisition of undesirable behaviors such as a prison of any jurisdiction. Although innocent people are given a demeaning life, physical structure and inhumane treatment.

A day in prison: it begins with waking up at five or six in the morning, with a shout "roll call!" Quickly you have to get up and stand in line and tell the officer your prisoner identification number. After the roll call comes breakfast, in the case of high security inmates they take breakfast to their cell, later comes another roll call at noon, some sporting or cultural activity, going out to the patio, lunch, then a bath, dinner, roll call and sleep. The isolated inmates invent headaches so that they take them to the infirmary for a pill or look for any way to get out of the fence for a moment, because confinement is hellish, you feel that the walls are swallowing you, that the cassette tape is going to disappear. burning for so many laps, it was not my case, but that is what the inmates with a long stay in prison expressed to me.

When a prisoner is left alone in his cell, the first thing he encounters is himself, with the voice inside him that initiates a cascade of troubles, questions that he has to answer in an existential way, in those dungeons there were unfortunates who They cried, they lamented their past, they screamed madly, others asked for sedatives to stay drugged, many choose to hang themselves by hanging from the bars with sheets and others are tempered like metal, prison does nothing for them, still others choose to read and the encounter with themselves, having the creativity to write a book and read what they can;

Undoubtedly, productivity prevents inmates from falling into the vicious circle of remorse of conscience, which is why it is painful to remain in a maximum security area, since there is segregation and isolation.

After the day's activity comes another identical day, a canine-like life. That is why psychologists have a lot of work in prisons, in these many of the professionals lack professional ethics, they do what they want and do not dedicate effort to their work and treatment of the inmates, they all detect syndromes and all they have pathologies, their opinions are obtained from the informative part of the captors, from any agent who stamps their ideas on an informative part at will, in this way the inmates are treated according to what the police report expresses; the lies and abuses of the agents have many innocent people serving sentences that do not correspond to them; many times by magic the person responsible appears, they assign the weapons to the taste of the captors and they usually put high calibers to affect the poor unfortunate.

It is said about the detainees that they are going to eat for free, with a criminal profile it is a high cost, the hell lived in a prison does not retaliate, the benefits received in these hell centers spend their lives. Any data in the profile of the analyzed prisoner is invested in a way contrary to the prisoner, the professional student of the human mind adjudicates pathologies that determine his future life. These ragged poor are qualified in an unhealthy situation, reliable results will never be obtained due to the situation itself, it is a sick environment. Undoubtedly, there are those who manage to develop scientific methods in their professional life, which help them understand the behavior of criminals, however, life in prison is not the totality of the factors to be studied, one has to go to social environments, family, political, economic and, above all, the prevailing social unconscious, everything analyzed would give a more confident answer.

In prisons there are fifty percent, if not more, of the detainees and defendants who are innocent, while high-ranking criminals or true transgressors of the law are committing crimes in social life, especially in abundance government palaces, in companies and public service instances. They treat the poor pichicato as they want, they give him justice if they want, they listen to him when they want, falling on him all the wrath of the law and consequently destroying his life. The mid-level criminals, such as the small square bosses who are dedicated to doing the dirty and bloody work along with the hitmen and hawks, are dedicated to doing the lowest work, while the administrative bosses enjoy anonymity and money. Living with the burden of conscience as do the bloodthirsty who tear apart and undo people with acid, pits or feeding them to their pets, this is a burden.

In one of the conversations with a criminal in prison, he exposed how he had undone many unfortunates who fell into his wrath, he murdered them and poured them into acid, leaving only a cream at the bottom of the acid container. The burden of conscience is not for the insensitive, who resemble beasts, but is typical of people with a scale of values and ideals that their social environment has taught them, that is why we are the product of being social. In prison you find those who handle crime as something that makes them proud and gives them prestige as a criminal, however, it is something very denigrating. It is even uncomfortable to hear them pray with great care to the god they profess, that the Pope canonizes them by listening to them. God does not listen to the innocent, I imagine that with less reason he would listen to the prayers of a being who behaves with his fellow men like a true animal. These true criminals carry the multiple criminal behaviors that, although they do not generate a conscience, it does generate a disease that torments them daily.

The crime business is in the high command, in those below it is only the first rung in the criminal organization, the succulent remuneration is at the top of the organizations, whether criminal, governmental or political. The reality of corruption in Mexico is in the bowels of each government agency, in the ecclesiastical elites, in the political parties, they are as united as their very expression of social control, they are a polygamy, all sectors of the system lend themselves, society is helpless. I am saying this based on the news, the cases of corruption and the corruption that we see daily, the government is part of the problem, because the big criminals have their participation at the top of the system, it is where billions are laundered of dollars, such is the case and clear example of García Luna. To launder large fortunes, there is participation of the high command of the government, they hire shell companies in order to launder money and simulate the provision of services and they are left with large fortunes.

Let's imagine a farmer unprotected against this rotten system, falling into a justice system that does everything but do its duty, it's like when a sheep falls into a pen of wolves. In the same way you see a town hall in the hands of mañana, or any citizen who is affected by crime, we feel like we are in a corral where wolves roam, selecting victims and swallowing whatever chickens they want. Delinquencies have benefits in the municipalities through the control of public works, the extortion of councilors, the usurpation of the police, public offices and jobs. In the same way, companies are victims, they make them pay quotas, they force them to launder fortunes and worst of all, they are left with the burden of the treasury.

The life of people must be governed by balance in all its spheres, the human composition is made up of real or objective material aspects and subjective ones; in the first, that is, in the real ones, it includes what we can see, touch and perceive of people, according to the material and behavioral expression of itself; In the second aspect we have the spirit as the motor expression of his body, it is in charge of giving guidelines for its existence and planning the other aspects of the person, as spirit we understand the product of the material organ called the brain, it controls all the aspects and activities of the senses and therefore all the expressions of the subject.

Next we have the sphere of the heart, this is a sixth sense and it gives us signals that are sent to the command center, being the brain, the heart is also material and works with energy, just like the first organ, we have the five primary senses As receivers of the exterior, these are the shapers of the material sphere and the subjective is much more complex because it originates in the act, in acting, existing, the essence of people, their history and ancestral information, their spiritual genetics, All that metaphysical information that the spirit keeps, that information that makes it act correctly or incorrectly, is a codification of values that the subject has awakened and leads him to the conscious, this product of education and awareness at home and at work. abroad. When the individual goes deeper into himself, he does not go further than knowing himself and therefore he deduces love for the great creator of the universe in himself and in everything that surrounds him. These impressions from the outside do nothing more than bring priorities to the forefront and if the individual allows it, he will have superfluous and banal things among his priorities.

The moral codification with the principles of duty to be well defined that give guidance to the central body to do things well under the principles, giving each thing, person and situation what corresponds to it, thus the individual ceases to be to become a subject to a function for the benefit of the community, the selfish elements released throughout the world, these are what make criminal society strong, there are functional families but in them one or two occupy the treatment of the others and sometimes the patient is the it guides and breaks down everything, makes "the family" a group of people without emotional balance, undesirable tendencies emerge from their actions; the social crisis is not due to being born bad but having a character that the social being determines and the needs, ignorance, mental damage and prejudices make the person lose their humanity to be a criminal, the social class does not matter, let us not forget that criminals like to be in the vanguard and in the social elite. Ambition is the worst of hungers and greed is the sister of crime. Many of the rich of the church leaders have command and money for favors they do to their parishioners and criminal partners. Thus we have a majority subject to the will of a criminal minority.

The essential doubt.

Every day that I live in the penal system, he tells me that I am a criminal, because I am in prison, because I am poor and because criminals call me that way, however, every day that I live I tell myself that I am not a criminal because if that were the case, the cause for which I am imprisoned, it would not be an act of kindness, but a mean act and with another result, is when I ask myself: can a person do an act that at first glance seems criminal and not be? Being that even the state itself has legislated in favor of acts of self-defense, acts of God and force majeure; Self-defense is a legitimate right when faced with a real, current, imminent aggression and to the detriment of the one who is being affected or affecting someone's legal right, these are poor arguments that I point out as superficial or merely instantaneous justification, but how prevent crime, how to defend humanity constantly? I could say in my wickedness, sacrificing the harmful and damaged elements that we manage to distinguish in society, not only the actor but also those who facilitate the commission of the crime, equally punishing those who cover them up. Criminals who affect common rights should be punished more severely, this is where society must clean up scum, but this has a commitment, equity, justice and fraternity, we cannot act in an advantageous and selfish way. Those who affect the common interests of society must be penalized with the deprivation of the legal assets belonging to the offender and his family. This is where the death penalty could be justified, when the criminal exceeds the limits and the price is life, when there is no other way to ensure the rights of society.

How do you know who should die? Delivering a reliable trial in which science, technology and expert capacity are implemented to achieve verification, that when the verification is firm, the criminal knows its end. Society clearly knows who are criminals, we know where they live and who their accomplices are, therefore, it is not difficult to distinguish them, therefore, forming a court of death that decides the fate of offenders, their property and their partners in crime.

It is unbearable to listen to the confessions of the criminals, how they murder the tied-up victims, with coup de grace, slit their throats with their mouths tied and their hands tied, in the same way they describe how they hit people hard on the head and impregnate them so that at wake up from fainting to suffocate and die, they point out in great detail how they transport the dead in truck boxes, up to fifteen piled up and stop to fill up on gasoline, how the gasoline dispatchers see the dead and nobody says or does anything, this This is described by one of the Zetas locked up here in federal prison, he talks about it to one of the Michoacan family who asks questions: How do you detach his head? He replies: "I detach the vertebrae with a saw knife or with an ax and put them on the pickcop so they don't stain the closed truck with blood. We have left people in the truck in the sun for up to six days, by telling you The smell is unbearable, but those who are going to throw away the dead facts and throw them in the sink, those who are going to burn the entire shells, only take care of tearing them apart for deliveries in black bags with pieces of the dead."

What is painful is the cynical way of saying these atrocities and after this, five or ten minutes of listening to these brutalities from the same mouth, you hear: "good night everyone, may God bless you!" these otherwise-sounding blessings are not gratefully received. Among the comments of the defendant from the Michoacan family, a person of same-sex sexual taste and the Z that does not look very well defined because it shows zeal when many inmates want the first one; These comment on the letters from their families, they are the ones who write them beautiful thoughts and in reality they do send thoughts copied from the internet or plagiarized from a book, in the same way they send them praise, but delving into the investigation, we found out that the same people introduced the same people into the roots. writers, cocaine and parakeet for those who are being prosecuted and the courts themselves allowed for the amount of two thousand pesos a day of cover, for introducing alcohol, drugs and special food; nice justice system It is difficult to hear so much brutality from criminals and so much hypocrisy, painfully for those of us who have not committed crimes, their "god" gives them better results than ours, which we ask in secret and with our hearts. They with the same feeling that they say they want or have the desire to kill tied up with that same feeling and heart ask God, but this seems to claim our God, but it is not like that, I have thought that God does not interfere in human affairs and if they have a better reach of justice is because the criminal world or system favors them.

Some of the common characteristics among criminals are their ordinary way of being and acting, infidelity, disloyalty, addiction, their fondness for exotic tastes and gambling, the taste for luxuries, the high degree of fanaticism and ignorance, greed, greed, psychosis, delusions and mental imbalances, project bad energy, most are pathetic; these being the points of coincidence in the profile of ordinary criminals, although there are many who can reach an apparent category and simulated finesse. In addition, they are distinguished by brutality, cowardice, laziness and their addiction to drugs makes them activate in the negative.

In Mexico we have the most bloodthirsty and dangerous cartels, we could list several, but it is not typical of organized crime, public servants in state security corporations also commit brutality and cruelty. In prisons, truths that hurt are heard from the crap that exists in the streets, institutions and on billboards. Thus, we can point out only what we hear from the cartels, most of them charge a flat or a place, extort, kidnap, kidnap, make people disappear, charge a fee for trade and business, usurp functions of the population, dismember, intimidate and corrupt corporations. However, I remind you that I am alone in this cell because I am in high security, they keep me in the cell called "freezers" or "coolers" their size is 1.50 by 2.20 meters, I only have a notebook and a pen for company That's why I justify myself if I don't have access to information and research.

We are not going to single out anyone to avoid a misfortune in my life, assets and family, but I cannot bear such baseness when I find myself among highly dangerous criminals being a self-defense, a vigilante, that is why I have to keep silent. The first thing the inmates do when they go to prison is ask if you belong to a cartel or a clique or gang. I said I was independent, but they related me to this "Mencho" even though I told them that I had a supply of weapons, they told me that if I was from Michoacán and was not with the Knights Templar then it belonged to "mencho". The inmates then pull their people to form corporations inside the jail, it is divided into cartels and also into racial cliques, in this prison we have "the paisas" with greater force and "the Aztecs", these are two gangs that fight for territory , some are southern and others are northern, others are "13" and others are listed as "18", deep down they are racism, crime and drug addiction. These people say that they have made money quickly through the misfortune of other unfortunate people, from whom they take everything and in an apparently legal way, take them to the notary so that they transfer all their assets, destroy businesses, companies and corrupt authorities, acting in a herd like jackals they go after their prey and take everything from it. This generates uncertainty in our country, generates lack of interest for foreign capital due to the insecurity that prevails. It does not guarantee prosperity in business. That is why the territories where the cartels are less violent, companies are attracted and society enjoys the benefits. The posters of the old school, maintained a line, a respect for society, today the tricks are a mean expression of the posters, they do not maintain principles. Mexico from being a trafficker becomes a consumer and that is when the lack of control arises, the addicts generate the problem, especially in the consumption of synthetic drugs that destroy the person more quickly, drying up the brain and the body, making them problem people: thieves, parasites, murderers, prostitutes, scourges, etc.

Any illegal act against one or more people is a violation not only of the law, but also of morality and against divine laws.

There are people who, without owing, fearing or deserving it, fall into the wickedness of one or more thugs, regardless of whether it is a government; With reference to this, if it is a fair government, in favor of the people, which acts in accordance with equity, equality, justice, democracy, freedom and does not deserve any rebellion against it. Otherwise, if it is a tyrannical government and the people have justified cause, they can overthrow, abolish and destroy that form of government and seek popular representation; there is no place for a person who is ambitious for power to harm the good of others for the mere fact of having money, power or property.

In the past of nations there are many examples of bad governments that favor systems of slavery, tyranny and against humanity; As an act against the person, it includes physical and moral damage to their assets, their rights, their environment and present and future conditions of well-being. It can be an act or omission, therefore, to stop doing something knowing that something could happen and you do not avoid it or do it for the best, is a violation, as well as to stop doing something that, if you do not do it, causes harm or harm, is a violation. and deserves punishment.

This is how scientists commit acts and omissions against humanity, by applying science in experiments that affect or alter nature and over time the physiognomy of some people, the genetic alteration of people and plants, animals, viruses, bacteria and others in an irresponsible way is an attack against humanity, it is equally evil, the alloying of elements for criminal purposes, as long as the alloys are not for purposes of production, construction and progress. The bacteria used to exterminate a race. To harm its technology, to unbalance a country and generate crisis and rejection of its production, that is a terrorist crime; it is possible to say that no, the economic factor is the one that moves, determines and bases the acts of the majority of humanity and there is little room for acts of love, altruism, service and benevolence in the behavior of people, the world is moves for the money symbol; maternal love, between parents, siblings, is becoming merely a mechanical and mercantile relationship, of suppliers, creditors and debtors; merely bland behaviorism in which there is similarity to any other animal race on the planet. How to foster love? Love is the most beautiful and pure feeling in human nature and is not only received, but is built from the person himself and is from the age of pregnancy until the person dies, parents are the main responsible for sowing love in their children.

The system itself is a cruel, ruthless system, it is merely a constant competition, a devouring world, in which devourers and devoured are included, at any moment the opponent's strength becomes superior and we are destroyed of our status, role and atrophied. life is mostly a world of devoured, a world without love and without compassion for anyone; the price of a mistake or the price of a success can cost us our lives, if the loss of climbing in the world of predators goes well, however it must be said that we are not ordinary animals, we have the capacity to govern ourselves under the regime of reason and reasonableness, in a world where predators do not exist and we are all satisfied through human wisdom, technology and science, in a world that governs equality, equity, horizontality, work, the effort, virtue and not vice.

How can a people be virtuous? Through wisdom, fulfilling his duties to himself, his family and humanity, having a deep commitment to his government, if the government has an ignorant people it will be an ignorant government, if the family is virtuous it will have admirable achievements and will influence its future and its government. How does government achieve virtue? As long as it is a popular government, it will have a chance, as long as it is led with principles and ideals, obeying its people and with the commitment to permanently educate itself and educate itself, thus it will be a capable, virtuous government with the recognition and affection of its people.

The economy should not be individual or a monopoly of oligarchs or magnates, the economy and wealth is for the well-being of all, so that everyone has what is necessary to live with dignity and happiness. It seems fantastic that the worker has the ability to work in cooperatives, in which he owns the factory or the means of production and that his work helps him to be better, to have time to educate his children with love, to to be able to travel, meet, live and work to live with dignity, the economy has to be localized or regionalized, rather, it has to be popularized, where the person's potential is to produce enough for himself and his family, the The government is responsible for the distribution, welfare, equity, equality for the social sectors, where you cannot have more than one house, more than two cars per family, you cannot hoard anything; that the payments are the same for all trades and that if there are more members the family is administered proportionally, a world where everyone is rich or everyone is poor. The government be the people and the people be the government.

Therefore, there is no cavity for some to have a full chest while others among fish and without having a net to fish, what I would not give to have a better world.

Today at the university of crime we came across some surprises and peculiarities, from early on I was a victim of the bad behavior of criminals who are like heartworms, very annoying, during breakfast they begin to lash the micas of the security doors, it can be said that I I am in the maximum security area, "because of my highly dangerous profile", "because of my criminological profile", in this area they serve us "the trays" (prisoner's plate), "the chicks" are the ones that serve us the dishes They are employees of the "cosmopolitan" company that sells its food, laundry, construction, maintenance and other services to the detention center, and because of the yellow suit or costume they gave them chicks. Without forgetting the purpose of the mention, the criminals insult these people, in a reprehensible way, which has been commented, "let's see if they don't poison us", they are humble people with Otomi features and neighboring towns of indigenous origin, however, there are people who are respectful and show a minimum of education, thanking the attention and service of "the chicks".

On this day we received attention to requests from inmates; The prison is entered with the authorization of the technical council, so I found myself in need of requesting my wife's authorization and it took me a good surprise, my whole family is authorized, even my son who is born next January 2014, first God, and my wife is not authorized, in the requests made (two maxims) I asked to be relocated from this place because it is very cold and my lung has hurt since I found myself in this "icebox" (refrigerator-type cell). Upon returning from the requests on a waiting shelf, I had to chat with an Otomi indigenous man, who asked me a question: did you bring people? Immediately I did not know what to answer and my answer was "I am a private individual, I work in a transport company in an indigenous community" and he told me: "I brought people" that is, it was a small band of assailants; "I went to a far away place, it's called Chihuahua, I tried the fish and some gentlemen told me that you earn seven thousand pesos, every fortnight working as "la maña" and I came to my town and worked with people that I loved. I said I would earn seven thousand pesos if they help me and the municipal president told me: one part for you and the other for me, he assaulted the SEDESOL truck that brings three million and we assaulted it, killing seven policemen, that's why I'm in prison here because those who saw it said, but I was wearing ski masks and they say they were big cigars, it's because I dropped everything, I only have my shotgun left; the president from above is investigating me with some people that he sent to my town to investigate, I have a lawyer who speaks Otomi and he helps me, my first wife also helps me, I have two children and my second wife is suing me for child support , the first branded some cows to give to the second."

Then the prison guard arrived and took me to my cell or room and I no longer had time to talk with that downpour of just 1.50 m. tall, with oriental factions, it is true that we indigenous people have constitutional privileges but that does not give us the right to trample on the rights of people, much less if they are from our people, many of the indigenous peoples emigrate temporarily to the farms and sales of agricultural products and derivatives, in this work they earn to recover their strength for the next day, that is why this shorty was dazzled when he heard the amount of 7,000 pesos per fortnight for his helpers, of course, for him it would be much higher sums .

Ignorance does not excuse anyone, from a very young age we know what is good and what is bad, that he does not hide behind the fact that he does not know how to read or write; I know that life in this system of inequality is very hard, the lack is enormous and we see the predominant number of defendants or prisoners in jail, they have little academic instruction, very poor education, many come from problematic homes, broken families, very poor families. poor, they were used by themselves through the addiction to crime, through the dream of greatness and wealth they get involved and they are thundered when they stop being functional or when luck is no longer on their side.

In the confessions, I heard that the letter cartel is in decline, it's because this cartel has thousands of its members in prison, who point at each other, fight between herds and kill each other, in the end they walk the streets pure scourge commanders that what they do is lose ground, put an asshole in a position that requires intelligence, it is obvious that things will not end well.

Thus, the prisons are filling up with parasites who have no trade, profession, or benefit in this world or in another, there are many stick-ons that express their cynicism by saying that they are comfortable in prison: "I came to rest", they spend everything the day sleeping and at night screaming because the death rises; it is difficult to bear so much pathetic, however, there is a very funny guy: "Teo" a 51-year-old man with a strength of one of thirty, I say this because of the exercise or "routine" that he performs daily, he is a federal that He liked the illegal and he entered from a very young age, barely 16 years old, to kill for pay and became head of the letter, this man is the rug of his dead and of death, even of those he has not killed, he dreams daily of the dead, that bite him, that speak to him and claim him. He is an old man who has had many love affairs in the teaching profession and in the judiciary, the teacher called him because he bought a bachelor's degree in something and managed to enter the teaching profession, up to a high union level and many teachers who aspired for a position passed through him, it is As part of institutional prostitution, he himself points out that the SEP delegate, the union leader and others, sold masons, domestic workers, street sweepers, etc. They sold them the position and paid from the payroll, thus the illustrious professors and those who have a degree do not have a job; With reference to government offices, the dynamics of employing are similar, corruption, influence peddling, prostitution, compadrazgo and other nice practices that are carried out in government instances.

That is why, the role of loyalty and legality to nationalist principles take second place and the baseness of the government we have floats. This problem is born in the person who offers and in the one who accepts or needs the opportunity, but they do not have the capacity to exercise the trade at the height of the social need.

Then we found that the group of judicial officers kept the money confiscated in the arrest, that the sailors only reported one million of the one hundred that the arrested criminal brought, which was not four hundred and forty-five thousand million from the Chinese, but five times more, They are merely examples, it has nothing to do with reality, government auctions or are never public, when the goods are coveted they remain among the interposers of the rulers; This figure was very useful in "the agrarian distribution" when the latifundismo was fought, the landowners sons of Díaz "divided their haciendas" into the necessary parts among their relatives so as not to be affected by the agrarian law, so the real owners continued dispossessed of their lands and destroyed indigenous communities; legal tricks are widely used by those who head the government, so much so that the people or their own race or family do not matter, what matters is power, having and many times, what matters is the persistence of staying among that false society of parasitic criminals that appear.

Both in the government, in the media, in crime, in the church, in the teaching profession, in the industry and many etceteras; Therefore, it is necessary for the people to govern themselves and I am not referring to an anarchy like the one that currently exists, but a synchrony of voices and words that agree by consensus to ensure true justice in which everyone has their own which and every what, where by education, age, virtue and others, is occupied with the role within society, the jokers, cynical then begin their discredit towards new ideas and argue in an irrational reactionary way that the new forms do not work and what would bring backwards, when countries that have experimented with new social modes have made incredible advances.

Mexico horn of plenty.

Mexico, a country with a "horn of plenty" figure, we are further behind than Cuba, Brazil and other countries, whose fault is it? Unfortunately we have a very disappointing history of conquerors, until 1980 the problem of fighting for the recognition of indigenous communities continued and in the 21st century many presidential resolutions are still not executed. In the 20th century, the people still suffered from the ancient, cruel and ruthless slavery in our country, the Porfiriato, similar to the world of Porfirio Díaz, who take root in power and a neighboring country that motivates with its applause the stupidities of each president in the chair of the pines; the harassment, dispossession, exile and on many occasions the death of indigenous people feed the pockets or capital of businessmen, rulers and criminals, so that Mexico has become a territory of looting, exploitation, robbery, dispossession and repression, where the Mexican or the native peoples have passed into the background, the common Mexican without original identity is common and current, the sleeping protagonists are the indigenous countries that make up the diversity of races within our country, which arbitrarily and by imposition call it Mexico and its "Mexican" inhabitants.

Prisons are indicators of the situation that exists throughout the country, with the tact of a researcher, I was able to do a good job and statistics of social conflicts, social problems, educational deficiencies, social pathologies, poverty and crises of ethical and moral principles; The funny thing about the grumpy old man is his discipline, his similarity to

Shrek, his protest against the prison system, when he was a recruiter, it's funny when he talks about his taste for horses, women, exotic and traditional foods, his ability to paint beautiful pictures, his life adventure; but his criminal spirit ruins him and worse still being the last letter.

With reference to life inside the prisons, I can state what I have lived in Villa Aldama, a place where it is cold all the time, because it is a mountain near the snow-capped Orizaba and the perote, in this place there are o criminal, it is made up of 16 diamonds o ED, four buildings in the shape of a cross, in each block there are three floors that are called modules, that is, each diamond has four modules and there are three diamonds, in the modules there is a punishment area , of special treatment in which the federal criminal code indicates that political prisoners and offending public servants must be, I find myself in one of these cells by myself, which for protection, are "ice chests" due to the cold and cozy solitude , in the population modules the cells are twice as large as where I am, however, in each cell there are up to seven inmates and it is said that there have been up to ten on the one hand it is unhealthy on the other, a risk of new intramural crimes; I am referring to intimidation, rape, forced drug use, beatings, quarrels, harassment and many more, in the neighboring modules two "caricatures" are heard that in these subhuman dens are coveted by those with compatible sexual tastes, some are left in population with more inmates who live directly with them.

I have referred to people who were born male but with different tastes (homosexuals) throughout their lives they become transsexuals due to the modifications they make to their bodies, injections, prostheses, etc. and it is said that some arrive in prison with a body similar to that of a woman and the prison doctors remove the modifications they bring, extract the silicone from their breasts and "inject them with pheromones", I do not understand why if those of taste Otherwise, they cannot be with residents of these places, they put them in men's prisons, that they place them in women's prisons in a special area, it is an adventurous opinion; the nominative of "caricatures" did not come from me, but that is what they are called here in prison.

There are men who embed silicone spheres from the window panes in the viral member "to be more effective in the sexual act, and to satisfy women", but those who do not have a wife and are sentenced to many years in prison, Why do they wear that? They tear or cut with a razor blade part of the leather or skin of the penis and they put pressure on the sphere or "pearl" in unsanitary conditions and with the risk of contracting an infection, apart from the complex sexual, criminals have serious problems with sexual control, with any image, conversation, sight of women, memories and homosexuals, causes them sexual stimulation and they say masturbate. It is true that seeing a woman inside the prison causes a sensation and attracts attention, but it is different from seeing her without morbidity, it is the lack of control and lack of sexual education that leads inmates to disrespect the representatives.

The criminal sees the woman as an object, a luxury that makes up the trousseau of a criminal, they see her as a servant, errand boy, supplier of drugs and whims of the inmate, even though she is the mother of his children and they lack the dignity and respect of his own blood, but who cares about others if life itself does not matter, criminals when they lack everything lament and curse others, blaming everyone except them for their actions. I am fortunate and happy to say that I am in prison for fighting alongside the people, for self-defense and because I live in a country that represses those who do good, they deprived me of my freedom illegally, causing irreparable damage, I am sorry to have I have wasted moments without giving cloying affection to my daughter and my wife who is almost about to give birth, barely a month old, I think it is a waste of time to waste an hour on superfluous things, when you can live intensely loving someone their filial and loved ones.

In prison you think about and value the moments that you lived next to your son, mother, father, brother, and you lament for every hour that you did not take advantage of to play with your children, I mean those who have or have the ability to recognize the errors and omissions of which our loved ones were victims, for me it is unfortunate that I did not commit more than a few parties, temporary evasions of the pain of living in an unfair world and the impotence of not being able or not knowing how to make transcendent changes in my society For this pretext and others, for pleasure they alienate another human being, but at the end of the day when sobriety hits us, we realize that life, in its pros and cons, is worth living and the best thing is put our batteries together so as not to frustrate our personal plans and projects, now that with children we cannot fail those lives that came from our actions and we must take care of both so that they have the quality of people. Because all our effort, defects, virtues, mistakes and successes, is reflected in our children who are portraits of our care and neglect.

In my case, there is a little girl born and a boy to be born, they are the anchors of the life of this prisoner who writes with this thin tube of pen and on this pale donated sheet, they are the ones who made me take up arms and accompany my people in their self-defense, against organized crime, these criminals interfered in every social, legal, political, economic, commercial and security act, so there is no guarantee for Mexicans, we live at the will of the criminals, the cartels that they charge Mexicans for every act, they are cartels that must die, so that our children do not live in that misfortune of not being free.

Our enemies acted immediately when the community police or community guard, self-defense groups, emerged in Aquila on June 3, 2013, on a property of the San Miguel indigenous community, land owned by Francisco Ramos, there were six initiators of self-defense, they summoned the entire municipality to form the group, to which the first day there were very few, in a week there were 60 armed members, after fifteen days he came to negotiate with the self-defense groups and it was a commander and the general secretary of self-defense groups to attend the visit, in the middle of the river, the sergeant-colonel asked us to lay down our arms and go home in peace, to leave things in charge of them and that in a short time they would give favorable results to our fight, to which We answered that criminal groups had been operating in our region for many years and that the army never does anything.

They insisted that we did not file complaints, that we file them and that they would act; "Very well, we will talk to them so that they attend to our complaints, therefore, we are not going to go home to be killed one by one as if we were animals, my companion was Vicente, a young man who was agile to walk on the hill and very intelligent, noble, loyal, cheerful, pleasant and etc. who was similarly hooded and with an R15 and his server with a 38 super command, dressed in a white shirt, on them a sign on the back "self-defense group" in front "for a free Aquila" a star that says "security Aquila" and with the rest of the clothes and the rest of the clothes according to the possibility of each member of the group, some got original suits from the navy, they were obsolete but they were original, suits that the navy asked them to deliver and they did so the self-defenses to avoid complications.

That navy squad that went to provide support to the self-defense groups recommended that they do as much of the law as possible; Eight days after the first visit, the army went again, in the same place, on the river, in the southeastern part of the property that was the cradle of the Aquila self-defense group. The requests were the same and Vicente accompanied me. and Ubaldo, both cousins to each other and to the one with the voice, we mentioned to the soldier the violations of our rights, property, people and our freedom, that those of us who were armed were victims and we would not tolerate another crime against our families. However, instead of offering help, the military surrounded the self-defense group with four checkpoints, one of which on one occasion surprised a delegation that was going to the courtyard to talk to a person and receive ammunition and weapons, we slipped away like hares, but a comrade said that they had arrested the leader and a certain Lupillo, so we left our weapons under a stone and went to the checkpoint, it turned out that Agustín and the certain

Lupillo jumped fences and hid in the dark among the grass, we We found out after turning ourselves in to the checkpoint, they yelled at us: "Mexican army" "Get down on the ground", we jumped down, we didn't have a ski mask on, just our shirt and they searched us, I didn't remember and I hadn't realized that in the front bag I was wearing a magazine full of shots from the super 38 commando pistol in my pants, the soldier grabbed the magazine from my clothes and asked, what is this? He himself answered with another question: a knife? I answered yes.

He asked us to get up, they gave me my cell phone that had been kicked out of my hand, and we began to talk for twenty minutes. During the conversation, we asked him to allow us to put our shirts on backwards so that the self-defense signs could not be read; We realized that Agustín was not there and neither was "the rented horse" and we went to where the mission was, at the moment we did not feel any fear, the adrenaline was one hundred, but after this came the questions, what if they had shot us? or stopped? Later, the government secretary of the state of Michoacán visited us, many soldiers were with him, the secretary brought the same speech, that we go home, that they would take charge of crime, that we lay down our arms, on that occasion, that of the voice did not attend the visit, it was the leader, an attention that in my opinion was very discourteous, rude and incorrect since he was drunk like almost all the time, he told him to go kill hitmen, that a three-year-old girl had raped him , his choro was so faked that it spoiled the possibility of telling the secretary about the omissions and complicity of the government of the state of Michoacán with organized crime, I noticed that the government left very upset because to close the short conversation he mentioned his mother and ran them to fuck their mother, acts in which I did not agree.

With the irresponsible acts of Agustín Villanueva, the people began to despair and yours truly was one of the first. I asked them to structure the movement into: lookouts, commanders, kitchen, sub-commanders, two secretaries, purchasing agents, general command and that In the town the citizen committee of municipal self-defense was organized to which they went or ignored, at a certain moment there was an internal division, for which a meeting and an oath were necessary, even though the leader in his anarchy did not respect, He was ungovernable, all because of his serious problem of alcoholism, your server, upon seeing a dark calm, published a first statement, which aroused interest in the press and in various sectors, from here arises the need to speak with our reinforcements, the federal police , who gave us warm support, then left us alone, for that reason we took the town, to strengthen ourselves and that's how it happened, at one point we were up to 300 hooded men and many women and children, old and young, the people supported us; meanwhile, our enemies allied against us, I mean the alliance formed by the old antagonistic group of the community, who were punished for "mismanagement" treason to the community, robbery, and many other accusations.

They joined with the provisional commissioner that was set up to achieve the negotiation because Agustín was not swallowed by the mining company, this group chaired by Fidel placed by Agustín his nephew in the presidency of the commissioner and turned out to be a traitor to his plan, they promoted an agrarian lawsuit against from the community, they joined the antagonistic group of the community that maintains links with organized crime and is the municipal committee of the PRI, they serve the head of the plaza Mario and Federico, they made a chilaquiles by uniting several factors against the community but their means were justified with their ambition for power and destroy the self-defense group at any cost, in the same way, the chiefs of the town joined and declared themselves in favor of organized crime and for this they received the support of the municipal president and his entire cabinet, I don't know if the mining company has lent itself to the black intentions of these criminals, apparently not.

Take the town.

On July 24 at five in the morning we took the town, we established ourselves in the command post, going in and out of the town, surprising everyone, we had no casualties until then, everything was going well, the state security committee was planned, credentialing the active elements of the self-defense group and allying ourselves with community police from other municipal entities that showed greater achievements since the municipal president was one more within the self-defense group, expressing greater solidity, direction, organization and strength; This does not mean that our group does not have direction and brains, but the difference was the age of the operation, a difference of months, in the same way we were burdened with the vices and prominence of a few who spoiled the order.

The leader told us that the community leaders would not get involved in the operation of the self-defense group and it was the first thing they did. In the group assembly the leaders told us that they were with us until then and they did not comply. The main leader did acts that they seemed contrary to our objectives and in a way crazy, crazy acts. Yours truly dedicated himself to the media, making statements, looking at the comments and analyzing what was happening, aspects that were neglected by the commanders. On July 23, 2013 we held a meeting in the place where we initially took refuge and five commanders were appointed, who would coordinate in council with the municipal committee, but due to lack of capacity they were not effective. I'm not judging you, a farmer doesn't need to walk these trots, a citizen of production and peace, what does he have to be doing as a policeman? Carrying a burden of providing security when the state is required to provide it.

Thus, when we took over the town, the municipal seat, the leader violated the agreements we had made, but he had always done so. Not getting drunk, he was the main one, however, one night he was drugged and he ordered several to get into his white truck and he went to wake up the soldiers, who came out dragging the rifle, almost asleep and this madman insulted them and demanded that they were going to give rounds. Due to the rumor that the criminals would attack that night, this was known by phone calls from some criminals; Meanwhile, the criminal group carried out its attack but from the radio and television from the city of Colima, the place where they took refuge when the self-defense groups took over the town of Aquila, saying that they were innocent, numbering 100 displaced families who with blackmail and lies before the In the press and in front of the government, they repeated the version of being evicted and filed many complaints against the self-defense group, especially against the community leaders and their commanders, the one they really wanted was Agustín, the one they had loved for a long time to overthrow power and they could not achieve it, although they did cause damage such as killing their treasurer indirectly, when he was president of the commissariat.

On December 29, 2011, the community property commissioner and their drivers, made up of Agustín Villanueva Ramirez, José Marmolejo Sánchez, Enrique Cruz Andrade, José Gonzales Jarcia and Carmelo Mendoza, were arrested in

Colima, in the PGJ of Colima. an anonymous call that they were from the pacific cartel and brought a stolen truck. Returning to the complaints filed by the displaced, they took effect when 1,000 elements of the army, the Michoacán Attorney General's Office and criminals who were pointing fingers at the people, under the pretext of arresting the offenders, disarmed the self-defense group, one of The crimes were the search of the house of Fidel, the provisional police station, kidnapping, injuries to employees of Antonio Ramirez, and theft of a truck belonging to "the San Miguel company."

The one with the voice was arrested inside the labor office for the crime of trespassing, but I was accused of stockpiling weapons and cartridges, I was working at the Lanesek company with Antonio Zepeda, without a search warrant they entered the company knocking down doors and breaking windows, they violated the privacy of a company and carried out an illegal search, they put guns on the two inside and only handcuffed the one with the voice, the companion fainted and they left him lying. They took me bouncing in the bed of the truck to Morelia, when they selected those who were left in common jurisdiction and federal jurisdiction, they saw that I was protected and they reclassified me to federal jurisdiction where they accused me of stockpiling weapons and cartridges exclusive to the army, from where I narrate my thought, I write a sheet daily, which I modify and when I am fully satisfied, I keep it in my prisoner diary.

During the stay of the self-defense group in the town, I noticed the disorder and made it known in an assembly in which all the chiefs were present, to which Agustín opined against me, I felt bad will from him towards me, I noticed that tried to imitate and at a certain point discredit the name of the born leader and figure of the community José Ramirez Verduzco.

That's how I resigned and nobody said anything to me, neither yes nor no, only Agustín said something bad about me, but that's the least of it, in one of the interviews with the federal police I heard him say: "I I am the chief and commander of this region", that is not true nor is it correct to say it to a commander of the federal police, I have no other feeling than to blame him for many mistakes, they helped our enemies to favor their intentions to dismantle us, they are these acts of indiscipline, lack of respect and disorder that I pointed out as contrary to the movement, however, he suffers the worst punishment, just like your servant, deprived of liberty, in the prison of Morelia, while your servant in Veracruz, to me They involved me with forty detainees from the Aquila community police and they framed him as a common criminal.

It is from where I have the opportunity to write these prison notes and I can learn crime at the university, not to commit a crime, because my conviction is freedom, respect and asserting our rights, so it does not attract my attention to commit a crime, much less foolishly, but justify acts of defense, if I kill someone it is because many people benefit from that act by obtaining their freedom, peace, dignity and security.

With reference to the criminal group, I want to mention their acts of discredit and opposition against the community police, before the formation of the Aquila group there was a march in which fifty people participated, "the narco march." 15 people attended in their vehicle and 35 people walking. The tabloid and mercenary debt journalist Ángel Mentis said that 250 people attended this march. The second march was attended by about 100 people affiliated with organized crime, threatened, hauled, employees and people who did not know what it was about. Ángel Mentis said that 500 people attended, finally, by not giving them good results and not convincing with their narco marches in which hawks, hitmen, relatives and instances favored by the crime participated, in their eagerness to discredit the self-defense movement they covered the junction of the coastal highway with the road that goes to the municipal seat of Aquila, in which there was a number more than approximately 500 people and Ángel Mentis received a payment to say that 5,000 protesters attended, 5,000 of the 30,000 inhabitants of the municipality, while 200 members were active in the arms group in the town of Aquila, men and armed women, not counting our children and relatives.

After the blockade of the road section of the Aquila - La Placita junction and Cruz de Campos and Las Brisas, the criminals took refuge in Colima, where they saturated the press with press conferences, newspaper articles, tabloid notes, far from reality, columns of slander against the self-defense group, the president of the PRI said that we had kidnapped his family, lies, his daughters and two sons do not follow him because his family is divided into Catholics and evangelists, similar to the division suffered by the community, it is a great majority against a minority, it is evangelists and ex-commissioners who promote the division, the landfill outsiders who enjoy the communal division because this is second of economic benefits from the mining company, it gives them contracts of services to the divisions of the community, because we know that it is a strategy, "divide and conquer", it is these hooked ones who do acts against the community, celebrating alliances with criminals of the stature of chucho Reyna and the boss of the plaza.

In the prosecutor's office in Coahuayana, complaints were accumulating against Agustín and his team, against his cousins and brothers for kidnapping, robbery, trespassing, threats and other crimes; this gave the authorities reasons to attack the self-defense group, at that time a young man was beaten and thrown on the edge of the town, the young man was thrown in a pasture and found by a community member, it is said that the self-defense group tortured and left forgotten on the shores. Another version states that the armed opposition group, that is, an organized crime squad kidnapped him and dumped him in the pasture, this person is a cousin of the cartel's plaza chief, he provided information, that is why one morning he was picked up, beaten and thrown.

They did not agree with the leader because he wanted things to be done by force, he pressured colleagues to remain in the group, under pressure and that was not right, this caused several colleagues to leave, they said this madman is going to kill and in effect, the order was to shoot the one who fled, he said: "whoever runs with it broke it" and pointed to a 15-shot 9mm and with macho signs he pointed to colleagues with adjectives: "mandilones", "cowards " and "pulled shirt"; However, those of us who were interested in the fight drove the movement to bear fruit or favorable results, so several women joined and helped, people helped with donations, weapons, food and even cows, we received moral support from various places from the country and abroad.

What did the community police do? Declare war against organized crime that stalked the residents, charged them fees, had them intimidated and did and undid; When the community took over the town, the hawks, hitmen, delivery men, launderers and colluded with organized crime fled to unknown places. These were the 100 displaced families and most of them landed in Colima. Where they shamefully received groceries "because they were dying of hunger", since they kept millions in their accounts or at least many of them received royalties for the exploitation of the mine, poor starving people conglomerated in a vacant lot in the place called La Capacha, in the city of Colima, we assume that the million-peso cars were kept away from the cameras, some did not leave a luxury plaza near the land, a place that served as a stage to present the work of the villains who they posed as victims, "the exodus of the Templars".

The displaced were harmed because their source of income was taken away: extortion, drug sales, looting and robbery affected their plaza, some of them have residences in the city of Colima. A clear example of poverty is the family that plundered the Aquila river, sold the land, sand, gravel, stone, and provided machinery services to the mining company. This family had already been exploiting the community's resources for decades and recently sold stolen gasoline and in an illegal establishment, without the minimum security measures. Another example of poverty is the former mayor nicknamed Car Lete, that man had savings of approximately one hundred million, a former mayor with very marked and defined criminal affiliations, this made him rooted in the SIEDO with the Michoacan, an issue that It cost the community company called Lanesek an amount of 20 million pesos. I limit myself to the examples that would fill my writing with garbage and that would make my manuscript less important.

Opponents of the community complexed by politicians, businessmen and former commissioners, contractors, city council employees who were somehow involved with organized crime, some community members involved in embezzlement and theft of community resources. In addition to doing acts against the common interests, such is the case of Fidel and his collegiate who granted permits to organized crime to loot the iron on the surface or boleo as they call it, from the property "La Estanzuela". What this group of crooks did know how to do was take advantage of their compadrazgo with the interim governor "chucho Reyna" (brother-in-law of the leader of organized crime in Michoacán) who sent his secretary to ask us to go home to sleep, that they They would deal with organized crime. It was he who sent his secretary to enter into an agreement with criminals in Coahuayana to file complaints and be able to dismantle us as a self-defense group.

Taking effect on July 23, 2013, such a hearing was held and he promised that in 15 days he would dismantle the group and it happened on August 14, 2013. The Mexican army, the prosecutor's office and criminals arrived in the town of Aquila, approximately 1,000 elements, indiscriminately entered homes and places belonging to the indigenous community of Aquila, beating people and selecting the detainees, stripping any unfortunate person who came across their valuables, stealing jewelry, money, cell phones, weapons , park, etc It was announced fifteen days before, in the process a false news came out that they had disarmed the Aquila community police, this without the events even happening.

The ministerial police remained for three days in the town of La Placita, waiting for the order to enter the town of Aquila, and they announced that they would enter at dawn to disarm, news that the man with the voice made known by means of the radio and in person. to the entire self-defense group, they did not give importance to what was announced and they did nothing either, the withdrawal order should have been given to villa victoria or anywhere. I shared the news around two in the morning and no importance was given to it, it was at the entrance to the office of the Lanesek de Aquila company where Octavio and Agustín were with their respective gunmen and they went to the orange, leaving the man lying group, that night I fell asleep at four in the morning on some cardboard, inside the office of the community company, at seven thirty in the morning I got up because I heard my co-worker and fifteen minutes later many trucks arrived of the army and the ministerial firing at their weapons, cutting cartridges, aiming at the community colleagues, who did not resist and turned themselves in, treated them very badly, they took your server out of the office, where he worked in the company community and collaborated with the self-defense group in the review of social networks, news, maintained communication by telephone with journalists and other people from community armed groups, wrote on the pages "value for Michoacán", "for a Michoacán free of CT" and On my page "Naranja de Valencia" and others managed by your server, a lot of information about the self-defense groups and news from the groups flowed on these pages.

That is how many people were disarmed in the town of Aquila and the expensive weapons were lost while they left us few high caliber weapons and they also stole grenades, ammunition and belongings. They took us to Morelia and documented us, they classified the people for the crime they wanted and left some in Morelia and others they took to Mexico City to the SEIDO, a minor was returned to the community, I remember that I They separated with Chavarín, Lupillo and Chente, they saw that I had an amparo and they sent me to the truck group to send me to the SEIDO, I only appeared in a single complaint for trespassing against the police station, an act that I confess was not true, due to the weakness of the accusation they accused me of other crimes: organized crime, collection of weapons, cartridges and chargers exclusive to the army.

Fidel is the uncle of eight of my cousins, one of them is the community leader, he was not detained in the morning, but in the afternoon, by helicopter and ground elements, as I told you, he went to the ranch after that I told him that the operation would take place that day. A brother of this leader was Judas, he was pointing out the spaces and people where to detain the leaders to dismantle the self-defense group. These guides from the opposing group are responsible for the arrest of our group and the death of several companions.

This group of opponents is responsible for the death of five indigenous compañeros from the community, they are responsible for the attack on 45 women, where they tried to burn them in a truck, where criminals set fire to the truck and tried to kill them, among them was my mother and my pregnant wife, an event that took place on the Uruapan highway, the absence of several parents in the homes due to being imprisoned or murdered is due to them, they are blamed for the deficiencies that many infants experience, they are thanked for the Restoration of criminals on the streets, drug sales and the operation of crime in our community, we blame them for the human losses.

Why do Aquila fight so much? It is a drug trafficking route and Aquila is a coastal municipality with more than 150 kilometers of coastline, it has the second largest reserve of iron and other precious minerals in the country, crime exploits iron deposits because they are on the surface of the In the same way, the looting of precious wood, apart from the fact that the territorial or topographical characteristics have all the suitable conditions to make a lair for criminals, it does not have communication or roads or the presence of security institutions. It has many slopes to take care of location and escape all criminal gangs, that's why the ravines and holes make the optimal place to hide from the government.

A much-mentioned event was the dry ravine" in that place the federal police clashed with those of organized crime, killing more than 70 people on both sides, although it was said that only 4 of the federal police died and six were wounded, the helicopter of The federal police were essential to prevent the death of the agents and the death of many hitmen. In that operation there were two community members from Aquila "la jumata" and "chilitos" these elements helped guide the operation, in the mountains between Coalcomán, Aquila and Eagle; Some of the dead were in an ambush suffered by the federal police on the flat coastal highway, in which the elements of the police died while there were about 20 dead hitmen, the highway remained paralyzed for many hours due to the confrontation and the dead .

The hitmen used trailers to stop the federal police units, on the coastal highway there are many curves and walls, ravines and hiding places, since one point out of many was lent to the ambush and the radios of the huts spoke to the hitmen, saying the location of the federal police, the hawks are essential for organized crime, since they are their eyes; Upon reaching this point, the hitmen used machinery to cut up the road, the war began, bullets everywhere, the radio spoke to the navy and did not provide support despite being asked via radio, this gives us the suspicion that they have ties to crime, days later a high-ranking chief of the navy who was going to Lázaro Cárdenas was killed, he was shot by the same cartel.

One of the most sophisticated corners is the private one of San Juan de Alima and the beaches of San Juan, likewise the jungle of the municipality of Coahuayana and Aquila, between the Chila ravine, the Potrero ravine, San Juan de Alima and Ranchito are hiding places of criminal groups, it was reported that a group favored by "pancho Pérez" who owns communal land from Aquila was hiding in the "la macarmina" ranch near the los mezcales ranch. Just as there are also criminals in the ejido de la placida, they make camps where they conglomerate, one point is the tamarindera in the intersection of the placita with Aquila.

The federal police were staying at the "las brisas" hotel in the largest hotel in the area, they left that place because there was a threat that the criminals would attack them and an urgent eviction was made from the place and the federals opted for leaving, leaving the community police without their support, unlike other places like Villa Victoria where the municipal and federal police supported the community police, being in coordination with the people, operating together; While it is structured, it is solid with the municipal transparency committee that is in charge of collecting resources for operation. Faced with this solid organization, the criminals fled to the hills where they were hunted and in the autopsy they found their guts empty and full of drugs. Having no other option, they took refuge in the municipality of Aquila, given the weakness of the self-defense group of Aquila, government dismantling and harassment criminal groups restructured in Aquila.

In clarification of what I said about the links of the Mexican Navy with organized crime, I point out that the Navy is responsible for crime problems, a hypothesis arises from the omission of the Navy base with residence in Lázaro Cárdenas, who were to verify and they made sure of the attacks or confrontation between the Templars and the federal police, how did they do it? They went in a powerful helicopter that, seeing all the action and receiving the request of the blue elements, begged for help to finish off the hit men, the latter brought very sophisticated and high-caliber weapons, luxury armored trucks. After the frustration of the navy. A federal police helicopter came, it made a sweeper and left the luxury trucks made of coal and twisted iron, the grenades of those federal avengers were fatal to the hit men.

The Aquila group detained a soldier with the rank of corporal, who was going with two hit men to collect a million pesos, money that he said was to pay the payroll, but what we believed they were looking for was to locate our people, since it was known that the military and crime served the same patron, Chuy Reyna; Hitmen from all over the state took refuge on the coast of Michoacán and that came from the voice of the corporal, who said that there were various groups of criminals in the hills. We processed him and handed him over to the federal police in the company of the hit men, then the federal public prosecutor's office demanded that we hand over his corrupt element, almost at cannon point they wanted to take out his corporal or tell them where we had buried him.

The information was already seen on the internet, we recorded the corporal and uploaded the video to social networks, making a scandal, we showed the video to the commissioner and gave them a copy of the original so they could see all the corporal's accusations, where he points to his superior hierarchs of having ties to mañana, among the military commissioners was one of those indicated as colluding with crime. We told them that the compañeros from Villa Victoria handed him over, together with the hit men, to the federal police after a friendly interview. Shamefully we find ourselves incarcerated today in the same prison, however it is one of the evidence in my favor to demonstrate the state of need and defenselessness in which we find ourselves as a society; insecurity that prevails in the state of Michoacán, thanks to that military man who points out that the Coahuayana navy and the Tecuanillo military base have ties to organized crime, that is why we can mistrust the government of Michoacán and the military, whom I point out corrupt, unfair, criminals and traitors to the homeland. The video of the soldier was made public on the internet and we published it from user to user.

Unfortunately there are casualties from community groups and many prisoners, they continue to gain ground, gaining mountains, hills and cities, they continue to defend the lives of the people who make up our town. God bless men of good faith, protect them from bullets and from the merciless and brutal punishments of criminals. Long live the people's struggle as long as it is necessary, current, legitimate, dignified and just.

The town is organized with "Mireles".

The work carried out by Dr. Manuel and some councilors is admirable, thanks to the work of each one of the citizens of the Michoacán people who rise up with anger and dignity against criminal oppression, the hope is that Michoacán will be different and free after the victory of the community police, I think that their example will be recognized at the national level and thus we will be able to say: welcome to free Michoacán! We can ask tourists not to be afraid to go to Michoacán, they can go without fear of being violated, enjoying the beauty of the state, its beaches, butterflies, lagoons, cities, architecture, forests, valleys, its beautiful warm and friendly people.

The other Michoacán is more valuable, the one where it is recognized for its contribution to independence, to the revolution, to the national agrarian distribution to its economy and tourism, to technological advances, that sonorous Michoacán with a thousand sounds and harmonic silences that make the heart happy and delight their food flavors, that colorful Michoacán dressed as indigenous and sheltered by love, fraternity, justice and peace. That Michoacán is built by the working people of the sea, countryside and the city, for them we must fight.

When the people have a popular body in the state with the strength that is required, its people will be happily praised, I mean the citizen transparency committee, which promotes culture, production, equitable distribution, efficiency and fair distribution; operating at both levels of government, that is, that it make autonomous municipalities, but with the affiliation of the state, that this committee work legally, scientifically and popularly in the organization of the population. Sometimes autonomy scares fools or opportunists, there are many municipalities victims of organized crime, others are organized crime that govern, they themselves charge fees or pretend to pay fees. We were able to observe the public works department, the municipal police and each one of the departments invaded by hit men, hawks, relatives of criminals, lovers and wives of criminals pretending to work, however, they do nothing more than get paid every fortnight. They submit to the municipal president of the party that is, sometimes, they put it. Doing a real simulation. Thus, Article 115 of the Political Constitution of the United Mexican States, where it indicates the obligations of the municipalities, is left without effect.

The delay eats me up if I give it wings, therefore, I give value to the saying of an old man who told me vulgarly: "hawk, don't lose your morale, let hope keep you..." despair could kill me here in prison, so I have decided to keep my faith and hope in freedom in order to achieve my ideals.

The legal tricks and violations of the rights of the detainees at SEIDO, to that department in Mexico City, brought the forty detainees in a truck from Morelia, with our faces covered and crouched all the way, if we complained Because of the tightness of the handcuffs or belts, they insulted us that they would hit us on the head with a gun, without sleeping on August 14 and without eating, just one meal, without drinking water, with fatigue and pain Because of the blows on the road, they handed us over to the SEIDO on the night of the 14th to dawn on the 15th of August around 4 in the morning, making us sign the declarations at dawn on the 15th, under such torture and unlawful conditions. appropriate and without proper legal advice we signed the declaration.

The legal trick consists of asking them for information, making them talk in a small room and asking them to explain what happened, then they invite them to testify and if they do not do so they threaten them, they are still haunted by the pain of exhaustion, not providing them with food or water, not allowing them to sleeping and spending time to time interviewing and harassing them with personal or group information. In this harassment, they take voice, DNA, gunpowder, anti-doping, tactile tests, general data collection and with threats, "they are still in the protection of the lords" and the public ministries that, similar to the dogs they kept in the doors of the SEIDO and in its corridors; Thus, without a lawyer, incommunicado, without being able to speak to each other, they forced us to do various legal things against us.

The group leader of the shady ministerial police asked each detainee: what weapon did you bring? The companions answered him with the caliber they were carrying and they wrote down the name and the caliber; In my case, the question sounded in my empty guts, and I answered: "I wasn't armed", and he replied: "You screwed yourself, everyone brought them here, write down a supply" – he told his assistant. He turned around and left asking the rest of the compañeros, who looked exhausted for 24 hours in demeaning conditions, terror, fatigue, hunger, sleepiness, cold and legal uncertainty; They kept us without eating until noon on the 15th, that is, more than 30 hours, until they gave us a sandwich, one for each monkey, and an artificial orange-flavored mini-juice. they threw some mats for each one, a few minutes after being lying in that unhealthy place, I felt a return to life, sleep came in a few minutes, my aching body and disturbed mind teamed up and prepared to rest, but reality was eating away the soul, however, the faith and hope that something favorable could happen lives very deep, I asked my colleagues not to testify, to spread the word, but the moment of the declaration arrived and the federal public ministry kept us incommunicado, He did not allow access to our families, nor to our legal defense.

It was with lies and deceit that they made my colleagues testify, they told them that after that they would go home, that nothing would happen if they testified and that is how the majority accused themselves, recognized their weapon and those of us who did not recognize our weapon accused us. collection of weapons, cartridges and chargers exclusive to the army, and organized crime. The public ministries made comments praising us, they invited soft drinks, appetizers, they were very kind, they smiled and they even grabbed their hands so they could stamp the mark on my companions, they hooked us and harmed us legally speaking, half of the detainees could not read and the another half with jobs syllabió. They read the statement over and over again and asked them if anything was missing, they made us point to each other, with photos of us and criminals from our region to prove a supposed link between the cartel and us, to the hitmen that we had captured on They squeezed with this method, since they knew the entire network of criminals in the region, they did it in order to accuse us of organized crime. Being detained is very cruel, intelligence is clouded.

The penal system is unfair in our country, it is a crime for the innocent, a danger to everyone, a way of violating the rights of citizens and a business for the authorities, there is no way to save yourself except with money, but if the enemy deposited a greater amount, it does not save us anything, a minimum of four years in the process and if the power of the accuser is great, we pass the full sentence of the accused crime, so we can prove our innocence, so we prove all the resources and judgments in our favor . The justice system in Mexico violates human rights, violates our fundamental rights, our guarantees. I hope that when our enemy falls, he lives the same or worse than what we live, they are guilty of suffering.

Procedural violations are very common in our justice system and the appeal takes months or years, instead of what the national code of criminal procedures dictates; In addition, they send the defendants away from the competent court so that the notifications take months to be made; despair is deadly in these places, they say that in CEFERESO number one in the highlands in this cold weather, many inmates hang themselves in their cells because they are segregated, in such a way that they are driven to death; I don't want despair to run through my mind like that, it's very sad to be in prison for the people who love freedom, our family and our country.

Let's hope that the oral trials come to improve our penal system so that in about 30 years from now it will work so that justice can be achieved quickly or promptly, meanwhile, we suffer the slowness of the justice system; Oral trials do not have the infrastructure and material conditions, nor the human preparation for such famous and copied trials, it is the novelty, like wearing a suit not seen before in our country, I can imagine in those trials to which we express ourselves it costs a lot of work and the memory to found and motivate us is not enough, due to little preparation, however, I wish the lawyers luck, little by little they will adapt.

On the morning of 08/17/2017 in the SEIDO cell, they made us sign some sheets without a heading, with the lie of medical assistance, to find out if we had been beaten and tortured, it was signed saying that no one had been beaten or tortured and after 2 minutes they opened the bars, we thought we were free and when we left the cell there were elements of the navy and the PGR ready to transfer us to CEFERESO; doing procedural analysis, the constitutional terms were violated and we were prosecuted quickly so as not to have time to defend ourselves, the lawyer never arrived on time, she stayed to assist those in Morelia, while the community members were incriminated as kids.

In the federal readaptation center they receive us with mockery and humiliation, they strip us completely naked, they give us a speech of obedience where with shouts in our ears they tell us the way to answer the custodians, that we repeat "yes sir" or, as the case may be, " no sir" did you understand? Yes sir!, they ask us to put our clothes in a plastic bag, later, they make us do squats, then they pass us in a line naked in front of the dogs and they put us in bags with beige clothes (shirt, pants, shirt, jacket , shoes, socks and breeches), they take pictures of us, they order us to put on shorts and pants to cut our hair, they force us to shave dry, some comrades with thick beards were crying blood, those ordinary razors were not enough, afterwards of this affront and destruction of dignity, the breach of honor and moral damage; They take us to the separations, a building for the new ones, for those who have a constitutional term of 144 hours and later transfer them to the town or to the ice chests.

After all, a plea from the inmate to accept the entry of the visit, but his relatives and the visiting spouse face a long list of bureaucratic requirements and, even worse, if the spouse is a concubine instead of a spouse, they are forced to to demonstrate the concubinage through a voluntary jurisdiction trial before the family judge in civil matters, which takes from 3 to 6 months, otherwise, it is to make a marriage contract, just as your server did, while in prison I married my wife, I gave her instructions on how to process the marriage and she signed it a couple of days before me, so we did not get married on the same date, although on paper it says that we got married on the same date day, in this way the process of entering the maximum security prison can be expedited.

You see what life is like in a small town, they said that my wife offered me marriage, so I realize that the arguende is tasty. The visit, after being accepted, waits for the scheduled day and shows up at the prison for admission, it seems simple, after they humiliate the women with a characteristic despotism in the prison guards, it goes through the lightning filter x, the dog filter, the nude filter and at all times, they are checking it visually; When the visit ends, the inmates are taken to a bathroom and they undress him item by item, they check everything and pass the dog around so that it sniffs everything, then they crouch the prisoner down and pass a metal detector through his butt and belly They check his penis and to finish they make him do 3 naked squats and, in the third one, he remains squatting and coughs three times, after he opens his mouth and changes clothes.

Today is my wife's first visit, they had not authorized her and they could do so since September 30; I feel very good in the aspect that I had already gone more than 2 months without seeing my wife and without hearing from my family, that is why I feel without 10 kg of despair and worry. today I know that everyone is fine and that my son will be born in less than a month and my daughter already talks more and that she still remembers me and points out dad in the photos that at her year and a half she is affectionate and gives kisses to her moms (to my mom and my granny help) and to the baby's belly, the visit is like a glass of fresh flavored water in the sunny desert, whoever doesn't try that glass of water always feels thirsty, it's because they don't have nobody or because the economic possibilities of visiting are very few or nil, my wife spent 24 hours of travel to come see me and the money of 2 weeks worked by your server, while she earned 2000 MXN per week, the poorest earn much less, a visit fills you with hope to continue fighting for freedom, the batteries are charged, a certain tranquility is generated; I hope 2 and a half months from now, see my son and give him a kiss, they tell me that he has a split piocha like his father.

The heart beats with great force when there is news from the people we love and it is possible that even a laugh alone escapes from the lips and the batteries are charged, the mind purges all that pressure that makes it tired, thank God! Because my heart and my mind are clean, because my hands and my tongue have not killed anyone, unfortunately we found out that there are injustices that ruffle the soul of my fellow community members, they tore the skin off their faces, their feet were broken, they were brutally tortured and then They hung them near their town Zapotán, they are injustices that only criminals commit to these 2 compañeros. Through their struggle and suffering, they have bought a space in heaven and in our memories, may God have them in his holy glory and use them in heavenly guards who he removed a hindrance from god who removes a hindrance from god so that his plans are fulfilled and wines gain heavenly acceptance to kill a criminal is to help the divine plan.

There are sayings of prisoners and ex-convicts in jail and in bed they meet friends. I hope to leave soon to thank my friends who have recognized that there is some friendship between us and we will continue in this fight, even though the government opposes it. Dignified and rebellious visits never live in our work, good people of our country live for our children and our children's children, I will oppose the easy life as many times it is presented in different faces and circumstances and I have refused to do evil to many people for the satisfaction of selfishness Seat 6 days of our arrest on 08/14/2013. At this point in life. I would say my grandmother.

No court wants to handle our matter, so almost four months have passed and no one feels they have enough authority to sentence us or release us. According to the federal Penal Code in its article 15 it indicates the forms of excuse of the crime and our matter fits very well in the state of necessity. Self defense is legitimate; At the moments when I start to burn tape, the mind formulates suspicions, hypotheses, solutions and in the same way thinks the worst, close to what has us in prison: a matter of politics, money and power. That's why I get furious when I think about the omissions of the authorities and the bad hearts of criminals with and without a license. At what point on earth did we have to be born? That all the time we are decades behind other countries: in government, in education, in economy, in security, etc.

I have faith in the judges and magistrates, I know that they have the capacity to understand the situation, but I do not know what is behind all this that deprives us of a legal process in accordance with the Constitution. In the article that indicates the characteristics of justice and the relative ones in the procedural laws and penal code. Those affected by a poor justice system are all of us who can be in a criminal situation, all Mexicans and foreigners who are related to the things and people of our country; the proposal and/or petition has been submitted to the Attorney General of the Nation.

Let's hope that this gentleman gives us freedom, which is ours, and they take action on the matter of Michoacán; Security is a problem that we all suffer from and not all of us do our part to solve the problem, security is everyone's problem. Today I confirmed the position of the criminals, regarding the Military, one said: they are the same as the judicial, Police and prostitutes; We agree on something, in the comment, the military have commanders and they are the ones who receive gifts, bribes, mutiny and commanders of squares; Let's hope that military baseness disappears and they become professional so that our country enjoys loyal elements, both in the military and in the entire group of Government names; All institutions are in crisis. Little by little, they believe that only the executive authority has big problems, or that the administrative authority is safe, or that the judicial authority is safe, of course, all areas of government have many problems, along with these problems is the rejection of the citizens for the government institutions, Mexico complains about its government and its government fits in with its citizens.

Sport in prison is undoubtedly a way to de-stress inmates and stimulate their state of mind. In prison I have started with sports activity, the first times I played soccer I felt very light. But I did badly with 2 tears in my legs and with my breathing, however, I played for a long time, the tears were caused by overexertion, I lasted a month asking for anti-inflammation cream and they never gave me; Here in prison they seem like politicians, they only take the data to avoid aggression or promotion of protection, but they never make the request. I continued playing the times I went out into the courtyard and inside the cells I exercised and stretched my muscles, even though it hurt and the In a few days the pain and discomfort were banished. I lasted four years without playing, after those games with the soccer team of the philosophy school of the University of Colima, in which the body seems heavier in the coastal region.

It should be said that I am in a federal center, high in the mountains of Veracruz, here the physical performance is greater than on the coast and I suppose that is why, in the regions where the pressure is less, people are more active and productive However, these people age quickly in our environment, because the cold keeps people young. In this mountain the cold reaches minus 4°C. That is why the cells where I am are called the rows. Here you learn to play chess and other board games; soccer, volleyball and basketball are played on the court. Inside the cell, they do routines, series of exercises such as sit-ups, push-ups, gloves, squats, etc.

What else can I do, one? Apart from sleeping like a cow, we can write some thoughts, songs, write a book, read one of the 2 books that are provided per month. You can draw, write a letter, and the rest of the time think and think. Some who are or think they are singers can do it, even if they later anger the cell neighbors. On a past occasion, an inmate who was in the room, lent me his file, it is something forbidden to pass objects and talk with others, in the file, I realized many violations of our rights when being incarcerated, one of those is verified when reading an amparo trial for denial of incentives, sport is a stimulus, in the constitutional hearing it was said and agreed that the prisoner did not attend said constitutional hearing. How will you attend court? And second, the responsible authority denied that it was violating that right and therefore the amparo is dismissed and the defendant loses being protected by federal justice, do me a favor, going back to the idea, sport is essential for people.

The fight of a social fighter.

A month after my arrest, my wife told me that a friend of my father's who my brother and I live with in Colima had died of cancer. My family went to his wake, this person's job was to be a priest. It was his turn to attend to the problems in Aquila, this priest because of his profile was sent to calm the situation. I refer to his profile as a mediating priest, he was going to calm the agitation that the clergy of liberation theology made in the region, a very good performance by the priests in this movement. They preached the Gospel as it is and the social conscience as it is, with this group of priests Don José Ramírez Verduzco participated as a preacher of the word, at that time the revolutionary church was next to the people. When the bishop found out about the action of the Church, he changed the priests. Some were excommunicated and like many preachers of the word, the 2 priests who preached the theology of liberation, with greater substance, deserted, threw away or hung up their cassock and formed their family.

My father joined a movement called the Unión de Comuneros Emiliano Zapara (UCEZ) and had many problems with a priest who adhered to the powerful class and preached submission, alienation and domination, while the businessmen stole the resources of the indigenous people. by signing a blank piece of paper and some alcohol-fueled fried pork. These dastardly acts were encouraged by Layo and the black, among other misers or fools who served in a malinchista way the company Hylsa Las Encinas, a subsidiary of Grupo Monterrey, owned by the Garza Sada family of billionaires;

they tried to buy the beaches of the sister communities of Santa María Ostula, but they did not count on activism, Don José and his fellow preachers of the word did everything in their power to stop these black intentions and the plan fell apart, the The rich gave up the intention, they wanted to give them 2 cows per hectare and employment in the hotel that would be installed on those beaches, I wonder where they would graze the cows and what would they use them for?

While in the community of Aquila they continued with the clandestine looting of minerals and in the same way they took all ancient objects of our Nahuatl indigenous culture and formed a solid framework, created by the church, the Community's directive, the municipal presidency and the company, formed the Union, Similar to the current mafia or command. They proposed killing the UCEZ leader of the region, that is, José Ramírez Verduzco, they paid 70 million for his death and five criminals did it, who were later included in the register of community members of the indigenous community of Aquila in 1990. Don José, was assassinated on 04/29/1989. The church is complicit in social inequality by its action or omission is alienating and comfortable.

When José was murdered, one of the boys who accompanied him ran and brought his pistol, shot the murderers, wounding Pablo's teacher and that teacher went to the hospital, they spoke to a priest to confess to such a criminal, as it turned out that this priest was the one who was the negotiator between the conservative and liberation theology groups, the criminal confessed and the priest found out what they had done, by password, he was not able to denounce them, we know that they have an oath of professional secret.

In our current struggle, the Catholic Church has been good. The one that does the villainous action is the Baptist Church with its criminal action and in favor of organized crime, the night before our arrest, the priest was talking with some colleagues and he invited me to be close with God and with the Church, to which I said that yes I would approach and the next day they stopped us in the morning. However. In the communiqués of the Aquila community police, which were typed on my computer, I point out the invitation to a secular struggle without parties, without exclusion or indications of sex or age. These communications can be found on the internet.

Social problems are not forever, that is why the struggles are changing and evolving. The current revolutionaries will be revolutionaries, revolutionized or replaced by others more rebellious and sophisticated. In social struggles, betrayals and unconsciousness or lack of understanding of the ideals to follow are common, however, there are those who know them perfectly, but their heart is bad, like that of a criminal and greed, leadership. Cowardice and crime are two inseparable elements.

What about the Mexican? Does being indigenous generate consciousness, rebellion and identity in the Mexican? What I am sure of is that the indigenous, due to their condition and historical pain, are more angry and their identity is usually as solid as the earth, its stones, its forest and its being. Its principles are fundamental and project its historical pain; the bullets that assassinate him for fighting for his rights along with his people do not kill ideals, although we still have stupid and malinchista indigenous people, however, the temperament and wisdom of the Yaqui, Mayan, Nahuatl, Purépecha, Huichol Chiefs is admirable, etc. Those pure breeds have my hope and my faith that they can transform our country. As long as this does not happen, we will live in a social mode full of abuses and violations of our rights and relationships or forms of social coexistence.

For many reasons I have moved away from the church in what many years of my life I maintained acceptance and belief, today I stay away from those things with poor meaning and great profits. However, no one recriminated or disapproved of their creed, we are all free to have the creed of their choice, I consider myself a pantheist without really being certain, in what I believe, I have a religion, I understand it as having a creed in something and that something does not have the phase of a Sacrificed father or son, what I believe in is what I live and participate in that divine, but criminals have greater faith than their servant, for this reason, because they believe in everything and nothing.

Day 100 in prison.

Language as a way of transmitting ideas in an imposing, arbitrary and mediocre way. Language undoubtedly has its origin in nature and later derived from the essences and by the decomposition of languages due to their use, comfort and hybridization of languages. Many peoples have lost their language, however, some leave characters in other languages, which means that the language is nourished and improved; In the same language we find many languages, if I'm wrong, excuse me; It is not the same language that your server speaks with the language that a lawyer or several of the inmates of the Jumanji house (the prison) speak, a criminal said that he himself told his criminal servants on the radio that they would protect the detainee (kidnapped), due to distorted criminal hermeneutics, a mistake was made and the poor unfortunate was deprived of life.

But how many times our brain does not spin the ideas, as the message requires, therefore, the sender and the receiver do not have an adequate decoding, I think it is mostly difficult to formulate and articulate, logically the ideas with some narcotic that is common in criminals, that's why we have many crimes and many brutalities, because drugs make the criminal insensitive and without conscience. Or with a very poor and insensitive conscience, without exercising the human side, yes, under the influence he is totally an animal, without human principles, without scruples. That is why they live drugged and constantly buy drugs from their boss. Who is the lucky one and the subordinates are paid with drugs.

When the boss talks about his company as some criminals call the cartel. They do not speak of the same thing that the errand boy thinks, the errand boy has learned to forget his human part to become an animal to kill, a mentally ill person who cannot control his impulses, a psychopathic patient whose central organ of gray matter it is polluted and deranged; That is why the language is not received in such a way as it is thought, nor is it received as a complete person. Nor is it issued with the correct linkage for being under a cluster of vices. We understand language as the set of ways to transmit ideas, so that with a look we can cause death; try looking ugly at an unscrupulous person, although we will only pray to a string of offenses.

Everywhere we find elements that distort language and make it complex. The noises in the language are components that make decoding difficult and the more noise the message or the sender and the receiver have, the more difficult it is to communicate between people and the results of the message will be different from what is intended to be communicated; the criminal's lexicon is common offensive and of little intellectual connection, although there are criminals who are very well prepared academically. The male sexual organ does not stop being in the criminal's mouth. At every moment repeat the word. The set of devaluations of the individual, even if it is not criminal, generates its devaluation in values. And it is done by an unscrupulous person.

In prison, skills are developed that counteract the lack of freedom and one of them is communication between inmates, but this communication requires security, otherwise it would remain vulnerable to the authorities, that is why inmate passwords and internal languages are invented. , one of them is the use of the Greek alphabet, derivatives of it and private keys that are difficult to decipher, only those who know the language can. They communicate with looks, with signs, with figures on paper and many other methods.

Mechanical discipline generates attention to the reasonable sense of the person, how many methods can we use to discipline ourselves, but one's own will is necessary and vices break the will of people, thus they perform involuntary acts that cannot be resisted because they do not have the force and get hooked on various irrationalities, such as crime, drugs, toxic relationships, pathologies and repetitive practices of errors. Indiscipline can rob us of our freedom by submitting ourselves to a chain of repetitions.

Being in prison means freely paying the request or demand for compliance with a law. Freedom is an imprescriptible inalienable right; without freedom there is no security because peace is broken. The repression is a measure of the State and crime to subdue the Mexican people, I say the Government, because I don't know to what extent it is involved in this criminal excess.

The mafias have their origin in the government, all of them have governmental ties, not only in illicit businesses, but in sympathy, favoritism, friendship, kinship, fear and debt. I don't feel guilty about anything, it doesn't make me lose sleep or make me depressed, much less I'm ashamed of being in prison. In a way, I am encouraged by the fact that I am not just any prisoner, I am not a filthy criminal who violated the rights of others by taking away or sucking away their heritage, freedom, peace, justice and social life like leeches. The cause for which I am imprisoned covers the feelings and lives of my people, we are tired of being in fear all the time. We are afraid, leaving our children to chance and at the whim of drug-addicted psychopaths and organized crime scourges.

At no time have we waged war on the State, it would be unreasonable to have an enemy of such size, it is better that the element of the Government that stumbles and falls be treated with rigor and all the weight of the cause and the law. I am not guilty of the crimes of the State, nor of the crime that has generated many conflicts in society. Nor have I remained in the omission, I have already stated that I do not want a country of delinquents and criminals who govern the life of the country, instead of ruling wisdom, freedom and virtuous men. The only thing that hurts me is my family. The one who has been left without financial support, without the care and attention of her father, without the support of her husband for my pregnant wife. It hurts me that my own race framed us and allied with the enemy, that drills my bones and spills the bile, it is impossible to butcher your own race, but if the end justifies it and the value of the Law defended is greater, they have to go, even if it's my own race. Whoever owes it pays it, it is a popular term of justice and that everyone receives what they deserve, the people do not deserve the filth that we live.

Day 102, Crime as a business for the authorities.

A grumpy criminal of the letter says that while his assignment as federal commander was pointed out to a pig thief who moved one or two trailers full of pigs a week. This means a lot of money for stolen pigs. He says that this guy acquired 100 hectares of fertile land, evenly, located in the state of Querétaro. What he proceeded to do was to collect, that is, to collect 25,000 MXN pesos for the federal commander per week; 100,000 MXN pesos per month, this is how the problem of rustling suffered by people in Hidalgo is solved, this is how justice works, the authority A lawyer said that it was not healthy to put little thieves in jail who commit crimes out of necessity. What other measures exist to solve the problem, so as not to make him an illegal worker. One measure is to tell your parents and talk to that person. He argued that, for the police and authorities, it is illegal not to contribute a cut to the authority. So the policeman, when arresting a crook, captures him and makes him his worker. If you steal something, you have to report it to the authorities.

Another criminal, a cocaine distributor, made his fortune selling cocaine on a medium scale. When he had his illicit business, he bought his houses, businesses, and cars. His life was almost settled and he was about to finish his medical degree. The ministerial paid him a visit and told him that he had to contribute a medium amount for the previous sale and would have to report with 5,000 pesos per week to be able to sell drugs. This forced such a seller to sell more and place more business; Otherwise they would take all your assets and prosecute you. This is how the authorities lend themselves to collect a fee and deliver it to the head of the cartel, in the same way they are used by the judicial, municipal and state police to carry out uprisings and kidnappings.

It is likely that someone close to the victim is planning or providing the information for the kidnapping. It is difficult for me to believe that the relatives of the victims provide the information and receive part of the ransom. It will be hard to live with the burden of having committed crimes against one's own blood, I forgot that conscience belongs to humans. The inhumane cases would fill many sheets of paper and the violations of the law by the Government itself is part of its operation between the illegal and the legal.

This is how many fortunes are made in the country, a place that has become a Colombia of several years ago. Yes. In a country ruled by organized crime. Even in the classroom it is recognized that crime controls the social, political, media, economic and governmental activities of our country. A councilor said that in the budget of the political parties he has the income or donations from organized crime, sadly it is so, for campaigns of the 3 levels of government and amounts are said. .¬

Today first of the last month of the year. They notified me that the second court sent the criminal case to Uruapan, Michoacán and the eighth court of the jurisdiction where I was detained did not accept jurisdiction over the matter and returned it to the second court of Xalapa, Veracruz. This will send it to the Collegiate Circuit Court so that it is in charge of assigning or defining which of the courts corresponds to handle the matter. They are playing ping pong with our criminal case. The lawyer who notified me says that this would be seen after the holidays, that is, in the month of January, if we are lucky. While the detainees will continue to be deprived of our freedom, our rights and damaged in our lives for as long as the calm of justice dictates a term.

That is justice in Mexico. My guts churn and I told the young lady that it was the second time that we were notified of the same thing. And that his words demoralized me and caused me to feel bad, later he told me to console me that the time of our stay would be computed, if we went against the sentence and if it was favorable they would tell us "excuse me, you can go home!" That was to fill my patience. The coup de grace What about my wasted time? And the damages?

I lost my second bachelor's degree, I lost my job, I have a criminal record, with this they will not give me a job, I have left my family in serious poverty and livelihood problems. The social affront, etc. To listen to those unfair, aberrational and cruel words. My guts and brain sink when it sounds: "sorry". Today I ask you for something to calm me down and take away this courage against the damn shitty system named for the administration of justice. My courage is that I am imprisoned for us to do what the useless government should do.

I am in prison for defending myself, for asking for justice and freedom they give me prison. And treatment as a true criminal and, even worse, they treat me as highly dangerous. Who should be in my place would be the prosecutor and all the ministerials. In the company of the criminals who feed their pockets; I feel fire running through my veins and in this damn prison it feels like a true hell, even though the weather is minus 3 degrees Celsius. I don't know if because of courage or because of the cold, one of my lungs hurts. I have not received medical attention and have begged for it several times. The Government of my country is a cover for crime and condemns those of us who seek justice; the criminal is acquitted and the innocent are made to pay heavy penalties. All legal literature and laws are just vomit of hypocrites and business of opportunists. It hurts me to bear the shame of living in a country without opportunities and where the unjust are admired and the poor are killed.

I paused in the walk of the pen and the surface that makes present my poor thought and my great sorrow to continue in these cold walls. The only way to escape them was through two visitors. One is an exquisite novel and the second is a historical account of literature and the worst Mexican poetry of the 20th century; In the first, my mind travels to England, where the novel was written, however, I needed something essential, imagination, it served as a ship to travel at incalculable speed, and we still have one more element, creativity. They provided me with my own England because I have not actually or physically traveled to those places on our planet. I realized that reading is the tourist guide of the imagination, it takes us by the Hand towards the instantaneous constructions of the mind.

This is how I built fantastic panoramas. Scenes probably similar to those intended or written by the author, born from his imagination or inspired by real settings. Reading is the only way to be free from prison; the way to free ourselves from the cave or cloister of matter. It makes us come out of the darkness and walls that enclose us. Our gaze lights us up, makes the invisible visible. About the poor Mexican literature of the 20th century I say it in a superficial way, although I see it intimidated, without freedom, like a mestiza, after being historically pointed out, belittled, hurt and devalued for being a woman. Enslaved in the slavery camps by a great tyrant with a thousand tentacles and a multitude of hindrances. Without identity and kiting in the dream of progress. I saw literature as an indulgent shield from leviathan.

It has been 117 days confined in this room, it seems that the hours do not pass, the days are cold, the icy nights without brightness of any happy star, only thoughts assail me, some make my heart race, others tense my body, there is no shortage of those who water my cheeks and those who unearth my teeth; The days will pass and the Government's debt to my family and to society will be greater. I do not finish reproaching those who parasitize behind a "heroic uniform" or in front of our people as rulers, when that dignified place or position is usurped by beardless, corrupt and inept, an element that has no talent to perform their duties and if they have it, they do not exercise it because they are out of control. Breach of duties on the part of the rulers who contribute to the reality of our nation, leaving aside patriotism and their duties to society, to their people and surrender to the enemy, becoming traitors to our country. It is so that I imagine that if the words that make up the national anthem had a sharp edge, I would cut their throats, and that, if that uniform that they wore was from a worthy army, its elements were not criminals.

Day 120 in prison, The geographies.

Geographies exist. There are international boundaries that make a goal for many brokers and the legal line of governments, crossing a merchandise from one nation to another, raises its prices, therefore, being placed on the market. Thus we have the trafficking of clothing, vehicles, weapons, drugs, people and all legal and illegal merchandise. Within a country we have several types of geographies, one is the one that is recognized as the territorial margin of a State, in the case of our country, within it there are municipal, communal, ejido divisions and large and small private property, without However, we can find the geography recognized by plateaus, mountains, climates, production and breeds; The geography that is not recognized or accepted by good people is the one disputed by organized crime, in that territory people are found as providers of money, goods and are seen as animals or objects that can be deprived of life or sold at the time it pleases you.

The chief of the plaza, the plaza is like a district in the days of the tyrant Díaz, the chief despoils the land and houses, steals the furniture of his subjects. And he threatens to take his life if he does something that affects his person, his company. This is how we have legal, territorial, criminal geographies... One side cannot take part of the territory of the opposite side, that would cause brutal killings: invasion, death, fight. What I have not focused my attention on is the war that Calderón launched and I have only heard that the criminals speak of this problem, in the war they put any filthy person as substitute commander for the fallen or imprisoned leaders, that is why they had many problems and loss of territory, since criminals have their statute and foundation anniversary, that is why they must have discipline. A war must respect the prisoners and not rape or kill them. Those were the words of a bunch of criminals in prison.

There are those who say they have put on the shirt and given their lives for it, since they do not deserve the appointment or the shirt, it is better that they take it off. In Veracruz prison there are many criminals who are not sent to other prisons because they would be murdered. They don't want them because they were the teachers in the morning, they do the people a lot of harm.

Making the publication in the media of the fall of a criminal leads to committing many injustices, such is the case of my self-defense group that was arrested and we appeared in all the media at the national level, on the front page and on social networks. It was a great deal by information mercenaries and when it comes to an innocent person they only generate irreversible damage, destroy their dignity and reputation and put it on everyone's lips. Publishing disgraces any unfortunate victim of the police, army, navy etc. The publication is a punishment, a condemnation, because the media condemn us before clarifying the facts and violate our constitutional guarantees. I consider this practice as a vexation, affront and a style of informative robbery, a practice of starving journalists. We will remember that the refined, wealthy class take care of reputation, let's say hypocrisy, with cloak and dagger; The false society is a victim of "what will they say". Public opinion hurts them a lot. It is a shame that it is said that they have had a setback and that is why, in the application of sanctions, the publication of the sentence appears as a penalty.

On the other hand, it is not shameful to steal the worker's surplus value and dirty business is not shameful. They publish the poor in all ways and classify us as villains. They display us in the newspapers and on television, currently on the Internet, causing harm and violation of our rights; There is the principle of innocence, which is devoured by the media business and by criminals who act as authorities. What matters to the media is doing business at the expense of those who suffer misfortune, justice is left in the background. For all those involved in this matter of arrests, the accusers want pre-trial detention or jail, regardless of whether they are innocent or guilty. Since they enjoy the imprisonment of the detainees, many times interests, businesses, gifts and favors are involved, which the detainee ends up paying for.

The victim of the system, in this case the detainee, is the counterpart to the system that accuses him, without scruples and without rules, they do not allow him to have an adequate defense from the moment he is illegally detained or "legally detained", the judicial they are dogs of the accusatory judicial system, they devour anyone without even touching their chest. They alter all the evidence, they alter the facts, they are not careful to handle all the information with certainty and objectivity. In events, many times their lack of preparation ruins their work, but it is what matters least to them, what moves them is robbery, illegal confiscation, outbursts, not reporting what was confiscated, thus, the riot is like the award. At the end of the training of the dogs, they give them their prize, their sandwich, that's how the searchers are. It does not only happen in the judicial system, but in the entire apparatus or machinery of repression and administration of justice.

Finding yourself as a target for the weapons of corrupt elements is to feel on the verge of death, the lack of preparation, scruples, training, formation or Academy makes the elements similar to declared criminals; The criminal spirit that governs the police forces and machinery of repression is equally dangerous.

Loneliness does not exceed the firmness of continuing under my principles and my ideals, I will continue under that personal regime and I will fight to continue in an ardent, coherent and consistent way; Criminals believe that to be opportunistic, perverse, advantageous, and treacherous is to be intelligent; Selling and buying loyalty, selling criminal capacity, selling people, buying and selling lives. It is the business of murderers, those who were bosses got used to commanding and many times, due to their poor education, in captivity they are offensive when asking for something, they are like hungry wolves who are constantly watching their victim, measuring all their movements, their possible defenses and their weaknesses. In addition, they classify the instruments that facilitate the commission of the future conduct against the victim that will fall into the drooling jaws of the stalkers.

Today, December 9, 2013, one of those wolves gave me 3 pages, with biblical lines and prayers, the act surprised me, that someone of that degree of criminality gives me prayers and psalms, at a certain moment my mind plotted and formulated many troubles . Could it be a hidden message? A notice of execution? Witchcraft? Evangelism? In the end I ended up reading the pages and keeping them, and that was when my mind said that it could well be something pure and healthy that is born from someone dirty and unworthy, but the content has to bring me something of benefit; someone told me that there was a dead dog, from where pure water emanated and it was the only water source, which was clean and healthy, there were two thirsty ones, one drank from that water and the other continued walking in search of another source and did not He succeeded, the one who drank was saved. These biblical pages represented to me that passage of the two thirsty walkers; criminals send their prayers to heaven with great fervor and preach the words of the Lord, that doesn't really convince me, that's why I leave my mind without giving an explanation. I know that our families, especially our mother, have to perform more than one prayer, for our well-being and protection; I have always felt a fire burning in my chest that does not allow me to believe in a mundane, profane way and requires an intelligent explanation.

I confess to you, it is not a trend, my faith is needed for reason. But a reasonable faith, blind faith does not allow reason to give explanations of the creed, my belief does not admit and moves away from nominatives, buildings and religious conventions, my religion is only mine and no one else's, there will still be many people who believe Just like me, but it is impossible to agree with words and the formation of identical religious ideologies, I am better satisfied with satisfying that feeling with a good meditation and a constant awareness that I participate in an indeterminate divinity, to which I complement, playing the best role that makes me happy, being part of that supreme being and being a particular of that supreme being without its own autonomy.

Day 120, The little kingdom.

The inmates promote amparo before the district court, commonly it is promoted by means of letters, they go to the judge to request the protection and amparo of the federal government, mostly the protection of the federal government is accepted and granted, however, it seems that it is at the disposal of a king and his minions. They manage to arrange things in such a way that it is favorable for the small kingdom and justify their violative acts; The doctors arrange their file in such a way that the loser is the prisoner; Psychologists invent their verdict and involve their observed in analysis according to the need of the institution; Analogous criminals say the profile of the detainee so that the prisoner is one hundred percent dangerous or totally healthy; The king says that he does not recognize the act claimed and it is not true, therefore, the promoted appeal is dismissed, so the king is removed. The prisoner's pressure and Possibly from the judge. What happens if you win the lawsuit? In favor. Of course the Complainer. The director of the prison mocks saying that the judge is in charge of his house, that he governs his kingdom, therefore, the amparo trial is useless and does not benefit the prisoner at all. That is why it is better not to promote amparo, even worse, the amparo trial raises the negative score in the criminal's profile. It counts as an act of misconduct, for which it is expected that the life of the defendant will be miserable, with punishments and violations of their rights; The punishments are: segregation or isolation, deprivation of stimuli, denial of visits, denial of sports, denial of library, denial of library and drawing, denial of medical service and little food. The director believes that we are animals in his pen, they mark us with a number on our clothes, he takes us out to the patio a few times a week and sometimes he walks by asking "Everything okay?" With gun eyes. Who would be cool? When you have lost your freedom and your individual guarantees have been violated from the moment of your arrest. Possibly there is a large majority of detainees who do not deserve to be listened to by any authority, on the contrary, to be rigid, harsh with them because of their real criminality; But those of us who are unjustly imprisoned, being political prisoners. I understand that in some cases it is difficult to know if it is a presumed innocent. The way to not waste my time is reading, writing, exercising, chatting with criminals and keeping the suite clean. I do this because in the end they won't even give me a public apology.

The king walks through the aisles and takes on the role of the peacock. He brings his cabinet and walks around watching the prisoners playing soccer or Zumba classes, attracted by the movements of the teacher's hips, that nothing and something is like a cake in the desert. The lack makes the difference, the need. The police or prison guards follow the example of their master, I forgot that those who act as slaves or circus animals are the accused, those who try to tame us. The jailers order some stupid things that are impossible to believe. It is a reflection of its owner who signed the regulation for federal centers, which contains a lot of stupidity. For this reason, the Ministry of Public Security is subject to a silly regulation. There is an administrative and executive authority, which is in charge of passing sentence and making the prisoner pay his sentence. However, until sentenced, they are available to the court and the prison only has the deprivation of liberty of the accused, who is considered guilty from the moment of his arrest, violating the principle of innocence.

The community members detained with your server are in pretrial detention, unfair and in violation of human rights and guarantees. It is said that there is nothing above the Constitution, but everything seems to be false, pure protocol and a jewelry shop window, in which the jewelry is fancy and the jeweler is a dishonest thief. I have nothing in controversy about laws, however absurd they may be. Nor against the people who manage them, no matter how stupid and corrupt they are. I don't want to think about what happens in the penalties that say they are worse. In state prisons, it is rumored that there are directors who remove criminals to operate in illegal businesses, as well as people disappear inside the prisons. They kill without any difficulty, they even have tanks of acid to undo the bodies or have land to bury them inside the prison, saying that they fled according to the prison team. It is life inside a prison dominated by organized crime, what I can assure you is the poverty in the quality of the jailers and in the prison system it is a misfortune for those of us who fall, hardly due to the bad intentions of the accusers. he escapes from spending a long time in prison so that in the end they tell him if he is doing well "we are sorry" what courage!

The system does not tempt its chest to tear apart any political opponent, agrarian, union, student, indigenous, leader, worker and for whom they pay the most. Thus we have a long list of fallen. Betrayal, advantage and in the same way we have a second list of political prisoners, disappeared, exiles and political refugees. That is why historical awareness should not be exempt from our children. I mean history from an integral position, not in the reactionary way in which they have made us swallow half-truths and what they have done is hide our history from us, the history of the people, the history from below. That is why they obscure the struggle of our heroes and the popular movements.

The example of Zapata and the Zapatistas of the 20th century and of course, those of us who consider ourselves Zapatistas, even though relegated and excluded by those who have the patent, encourage me to remain firm even in prison. We try, in our poor understanding, to follow the example of the great revolutionaries such as Mr. Emiliano, who represents the enslaved people, the dispossessed, exploited, robbed, repressed and starving indigenous people and the forgotten peasant. That is why as long as there is a tyrannical government, we will have expressions of rebellion in politics, in the arts, in philosophy, in literature, in the classroom, in the countryside and in the city. Today our Union of rebels is easier and we can easily coordinate from many corners of our country and the world thanks to the media.

The difficult thing is consensus, however, there are ways in which we can easily converge. One is the guidelines formulated by the neozapatistas, if I remember correctly, they are to convince and not to win, to propose and not to impose, to listen and not to be silent, and other basic principles. . During the partial defeat of Zapatismo in the last century we can point to external factors, one could be the socialist wave in a mediocre way, another, the US intervention in our country, even today interventionism continues. Similarly, the repression to this day, the government's repression of our revolutionary leaders and peoples, so we have a notion of dead leaders, artists, poets, writers, thinkers, politicians, and civilians in prisons the size of Belén, San Juan Ulúa, Islas Marías, La Almoloya, CEFERESOS and common jails. The painful thing is when our people are destroyed without touching their chests, like vile dogs. They tear our pregnant women, children, our soldiers with the edge of a machete, torture with rope, knife and bullet, there is no truce, the attacks do not stop. Today crime sees us as beggars in our own land. They take our comrades by depriving them of life, they rip their skin off their faces, cut off their genitals, cut off their ears, break their bones, hang them, torture them brutally, just as if the actors were animals, that's how we find our comrades hanging from the shores of towns, dumped in garbage cans, buried in common graves, clandestine graves and others never appear.

As long as there is a civilian killed by criminal acts, there will be reason for the people to defend themselves forcefully. Self-defense is not a crime, bring the weapons that are necessary, the people are sacred, the people are cared for, the people must be respected and there are governments in collusion with organized crime, they have to disappear. Those who do not respect the people and imprison their defenders growing criminals. Thus, in prison we have community members from different municipalities of Michoacán.

In the Aquila case. Organized crime joined, or rather, the criminals in command were uncovered. This is how the former ediles of the PRIX, the ex-commissioners of the indigenous community, emerge, it is discovered that the commissioner of Coire has links with crime. It jumps to the defense and espionage of the State Government, its delegates and links. The municipal president begins a dirty war through the media, the trustee, having business of mineral theft in the company of the head of organized crime in that region, withdraws his machines from the looted deposit and joins forces with his sister, Amante del Gobierno, her Sister of the wife of the treasurer of the Commissariat of the Indigenous community of Aquila, team up with the caciques of the town of Aquila and begin their attacks. They plan together with Chucho Reyna, interim governor at the time, who has a family relationship with the chief tuta of the Templarios cartel, their wives are sisters. They gathered at the funeral, for the death of their father-in-law, protected by the army, while the people were at war.

With the indignation of the Michoacán people, the formation of the Self-Defense groups was born, we have legitimacy and legality as long as we do things well. We enjoy legitimacy by defending our indigenous territory from an imminent, constant, current and real danger and we are endorsed by the people. The second, the law considers us to be protecting ourselves from threats and compelling danger, we are in defense of our rights. Our goods, our patrimony and our life. Who do we have to ask for permission to have security to defend ourselves legitimately. If the government knows well who the criminals are and what crimes they commit, it knows the criminals well. In the same way they know that they cry together at wakes. They eat together. They maintain businesses and many are Gobimaña. This is how it happened in the days of the highway robbers, they were promoted by the State.

Day 122, A revolutionary party.

The hijackers of the principles of the revolution and the monopoly of the ideals of the revolution are contained in a party statute and in history we find groups that congregated as political parties and call themselves revolutionaries when the revolution is not institutionalized, it is not patented , does not become exclusive to a group, be it socialist, communist, capitalist, progressive; The revolution is the evolutionary struggle to improve the conditions of those below, it is the stone in the fine shoe of the system. That is the class struggle that Marx prophesies, which will end in the dictatorship of the proletariat, a forecast that we all question, how it will be possible, and we also wonder about the possible systems in the future, of course, if humanity and the environmental and climatic conditions allow it and it is possible in the future.

We have those who in a certain way monopolize the revolution and make it theirs in books, magazines, media, clubs, parties, etc., these characters are used by national and foreign rulers to infiltrate and destroy the revolutionaries, who manifest and maintain that door open affiliation and recruitment to strain and flow information.

In my humble opinion it is to do a serious structuring of the revolutionary movements, in extreme security and high intelligence work. The structural model is held by some social movements only when they fell into transience, however, at the time they caught fire and that will give them retribution in the future; minorities will wake up and act in response to current needs, the current government will cease to function and autonomous municipalities, autonomous communities and protected neighborhoods will come. Against the organization we have barbarism, ignorance and disorganization, this favors bad governments and those who have led the people to mediocrity. Thus we have a first world but ignorant country that prefers to buy than to make talent. And our revolutionary critical minds are dulled with lies and with immediate painkillers, while the people continue with the problem they are claiming.

Day 123

We asked for freedom and they gave us prison, we asked for respect and they sold our lands, we asked for security and the bad guy joined with the bad guy to crush us and they deprived us of our rights. We ask that they listen to us and give us justice and we find oblivion, repression, jail and death. And we ask for freedom and we find political siege, espionage and surveillance.

For all our problems we must join forces, country and city as brothers, the peasant cannot be divorced from the worker, it is a lie that the intellectual secures his ideas in the social elite. It cannot be alone, exposed to reactionary opponents. The teacher does not have to sow antagonism with his students. The housewife should not surrender to an electronic device and in the submission of the cloister, live behind walls. The revolution starts at home. The indigenous person who shakes off that fucking suit that they have been put on throughout history, who dresses with dignity and assumes his role of authority in all areas. I'm surprised that being the best poets in Mexico they don't have production. It hurts me that, having so many languages in our country, we forget them and opt for the Castilian empire. The best indigenous contributions of America have come from our country and we lower our faces when they call us indigenous, when we are proud to be of pure race. The indigenous people of other countries are flattered, because a country with indigenous peoples is blessed; on the other hand, a multiracial country, without identity, sooner or later suffers misfortune. The problem of our country is called betrayal, they betray us every period. They betray us every six-year period, they betray us in the church, in the Palace, in the club, on the street, we betray and we are wandering in the form of our being and that makes convention and coexistence difficult.

Since respect for the Law of others is Peace, that is why we do not have Peace in our country, because there is no respect and there is no freedom. Without freedom there is no justice, without justice there is no peace, no respect, no security, and for this reason there must be rebellion and popular organization. The people are peace, the people are the measure of their Government, the solution to our ills lives in the people, but we have to endure everyone's irresponsibility. That is why we do not have time to fulfill our duties, to order our hearts, our minds and our families. The housewife lives alienated from the superfluous, the young man lives thinking about his next revolutionized radio or computer. The peasant linked to poor production, the professional worried about climbing a position, the worker lamenting the boss's abuses, the bureaucrat filing his nails and we all live crying, complaining about inflation.

We all live in fear of being victims of abuses of authority, we live denying high taxes, our low salaries and the high salaries of the rulers. We envy, perhaps, the palaces of the rich, we live in fear of organized crime and if you are not very soon you will be and we do not dare to take a step towards transforming action. Only revolutionaries have the right to criticize, the rest of us must remain silent because we do not have the courage to change, to say, to fight, to fight for what they have stolen from us: freedom, peace, dignity, identity, the respect, word, authority, etc.

Day 124 in seclusion.

Today they took a chest X-ray to look at my lungs and on my adventure, they took me out of line and left me in a waiting space. In the place there was a service cart, also called a little devil. In which, there were rolls of paper, toothbrushes, fine razors and soap, all this was assaulted by four guys who were waiting next to their server, in less than 10 seconds they had already saved what was stolen between their clothes. They assured an officer the task to deliver us to the hospital. The officer is crazy or at least sails with the flag of funny, among the patients was added a Cuban, who had 24 hours of having undergone surgery on one foot, therefore, he could not walk by himself to the hospital. From what the nutcase said let's go. The Cuban was annoyed and said that he was not going anywhere and that he did not want to be treated like an animal, that one foot would get tired, he chose to sit and not move, the guard told him: "Stay there until I come back." The Cuban He replied: "Don't talk to me like that, Pendejo!" the guard replies: "get up note!" We left and they told him that he would take a wheelchair to transport the Cuban and that was the case.

After the x-ray and the wait, everyone arrives and talks about their dirty deeds within their cartels or criminal cells; It was commented that for guarding for 3 months they pay 60,000 USD protecting the chaca from the cartel they cannot use any telephone, no radio and they can only go out with the chaca, that they frequent nightclubs and like the young girls from high schools, they also like to use fine and showy clothes while they talked, one said of the Beltrán who dominate the state of Nayarit, that upon the death of one of those above the cousin takes possession and begins to kill all the cousin's operational team, for not being faithful to he is something similar to what Machiavelli recommends in his political work, The prince, when the king takes possession of the Kingdom, annihilates all the servants of the old kingdom. They talked a lot of rubbish, cruelties, which all those who are imprisoned in prisons tend to hear.

The Cuban caught up with us at the prison hospital, they took an X-ray to perform the operation. The operation was already carried out yesterday, by order of the judge, the prison medical team is doing very badly, it is to those failures that I have referred along these lines. The prison system is backwards. 2 months ago they told me that they would take an X-ray of my lungs and it was only until today.

The Cuban was caught in Xalapa, Veracruz, for bringing 100 grams of marijuana, accused of sale and possession of marijuana and of the 2 crimes, possession was acquitted and he was left for sale because a person pointed out that he was a seller. That person does not exist, they looked for him in the database, in the civil registry, they notified him by edicts and he never appeared, so someone's intervention is suspected. The municipal police officers who arrested him went to prison, they are in the same center as the Cuban, so he is bursting knowing the injustice, he says he is going to close his case, and he is going to leave after the confrontation with nobody and If the judge recognizes his innocence, he will leave at the time of sentencing, but who is going to pay for his lost time?

He says that while he was released before his arrest, he was dating a young woman from the port of Veracruz, no less than the daughter of the municipal trustee. We will not be able to draw conclusions about who is behind all this, it will be the imprisoned policemen or the municipal trustee, something similar to our affair in which governments unite to blame innocent people, all for not having enough pants to fix their personal affairs by their own means they use power. To harm third parties, we only wish our Cuban brother luck. If you consume the herb do not allow it to consume you.

Back, the guard and the Cuban made peace, that crazy guard is cool with the inmates, he seems to understand them. At least that's what he says, when the Cuban told him the string of maternal acknowledgments and reminders, the guard did get very upset and along the way he was leaving the stream of curses and charging the walls with his bad energy, while some of us were laughing. On our return we were detained for a few minutes in a diamond in front of a security door because there was no one to open it, after a while a woman appears with a snail's pace, who instead of being a guard seems to be getting fat, calmly opened the gate and we entered for each person to go to the module that was assigned to them as a stay. The paisa who left the same module as me, loaded with toilet paper, a rake and other objects that I did not see what they were. But they make known the man. My mother, said "do not show hunger, even if they are dying" this in front of an audience in struggle undertaken by the Community.

For whom the ministerial or the Government of Michoacán sends us to Mexico D.F. It is a popular movement and as such, there are many organizations that support it, it affects an indigenous community and that is why we would receive support from more organizations and we are protected by international rights through agreements and treaties to which Mexico is a party. The Community can gather up to half of its population and move it to Morelia. We are talking about approximately 3,000 assets, that we could well move about 1,000 to Morelia and make the Governor sit-in at his government house, something that does not favor anyone. Because of the dangers, they know that the greater the mobilization in the capital, the greater the vulnerability for the state government and possible invasions. And Tomás from the community armed movement, I know that this movement is going to put an end to many evils in the state of Michoacán and it is going to win, I know it.

Then they take us to Mexico D.F. and later to Villa Aldama, Veracruz, to slow down our process, because distances prolong the terms and notifications. It has nothing to do with it, if the crimes are federal, Michoacán also has a federal prison, an intentional intervention by the state government is perceived to affect the movement of the community police. We noticed that from the performance of the municipal president, his staff, the trustee and his sister. The latter is a delegate of the Government of the State of Michoacán in the coastal region and for not leaving out the intervention of her lover Mario Álvarez, business partner and compadre of the boss of the plaza. Hitmen and plaza bosses move around in their vans owned by this former mayor and State Government delegate.

Lastly, the government envoy who named himself during the visit as the alleged Secretary of the Government of the State of Michoacán who asked us to go home and leave things at his disposal afterwards, held a meeting with hitmen and their relatives in ranchito and promised them within 15 days, they would return to the town taken over by the Self-Defense Group and it was that on August 14, 2013 they took prisoner 46 indigenous people and residents of Aquila and Coahuayana; In the same way, the magistrate of the Agrarian Court in Colima joined the attacks and gave the verdict in favor of the Commissioner removed from his position in previous months, for acts of corruption, treason and crimes against the community. They gave permission to organized crime to exploit the iron ore deposits within the San Miguel indigenous community. The trial 577/2012 promoted by these corrupt was granted the win and reinstated in the position of commissioners by the magistrate; when the community removed them and is autonomous, by will it can remove or replace its authorities when they do not defend their interests and commit dishonest acts.

It has cost indigenous peoples blood, heritage, lives, freedom, peace, culture, history and existence. Price paid to exist. The whims, greed, evil and corruption of those above is nothing, that is, it is the denial of giving existence to those who have an identity. They have wanted to reduce the indigenous peoples to nothing, but they have not been able to, the bad guys put the good guys in check and the malinchistas, traitors, even though they were of our race, they consider themselves foreigners, external to us, to our interests as common and We are commoners and community members who see for the good of all and we are governed by the principle of being equal for equals.

A historical reconstruction of the events will be made and the world will judge after assessing the role of each actor, in the community and it is possible that many of us will get scratched, but others will paint their past with blood, money and non-existent acts, those will be dealt with by the historians and historians I feel tired, exhausted and my patience is agitated from being on this fence and I would like to go out to continue fighting my enemies, for whom I would like to light a candle, in a few months I will go out and I know that I will have to take great care of myself. And I'm going to make it, I'll only have to go out during the day and to safe places, I don't want to leave my children without a father. I lived like that and it's painful, especially when you love your father as much as I loved mine, a happy man with many ideas in his head. God rest his soul.

It is the steak that whoever eats it needs rest to digest and have good digestion. What does Peace do? It is built by imposing their ideals and convictions. Violence is a means to achieve the principle of peace, but it is through ideals achieved by social consensus that peace is achieved and kept, repression only obscures intentions, it does not disappear. On the coast of Michoacán, acts of organized crime are being presented, they are confronting the north coastal side and killing people from the indigenous community of Aquila, taking community members from Coalcomán and Villa Victoria prisoner.

It is believed that organized crime takes refuge on the private beach of San Juan and also in the hotels of San Juan de Alima. It is there, in that town where 3 indigenous compañeros were kidnapped, in El Ojo de Agua there is a clandestine gasoline station, in that place they milk the trailers, it belongs to organized crime, next to it is a street that goes up the hill about 20 minutes is a camp of criminals. Between the hill of Fox, the tamarindillo and the hill of the güina, the criminals hide. The joy is that every day the community members are gaining the ground and strength that is needed to continue advancing, as the days go by they are closer to victory, winning the capital, the first battle has been won. They inform me that Apatzingán, Los Reyes and other towns have been taken, we need to attack. Before they attack us, criminals are thugs and kill when given the opportunity and advantage, they are treacherous. That is why they must be herded, as if they were animals, and hunt them as such, it is not convenient to hand them over to the justice system because then they come out and it is a problem, it is better to disappear them in the less fertile land or leave them to the vultures, which they will order, although I am not sure that these swallow Zozobras, matter so decomposed.

The reality is harsh, it hurts, but there are no other solutions than to end cancer, it is to annihilate the harmful cells. It opposes the principles of desirable conduct, however, we do not see that criminals tempt their hearts to treat an innocent or a community member, like cannibals they pounce on the person, torture them, dismember them and disappear. They steal everything from him, his heritage, his word, his life and the peace of his relatives, so they don't deserve anything kind.

How can criminals stay alive after killing with such cruelty? Very cynical, they talk in detail about how they dismember people, how they cut off their heads and remove their entrails and put their heads in their belly, how they deliver the body in black bags to their families. I haven't heard anyone talk about looking into the victim's eyes while they are murdering her, they don't talk about their nightmares because they're ashamed to say they're scared. Some cry asleep, scream and others suffer from insomnia, many are deranged and miss the drug in order to calm down that evil world that they have been carrying around.

In criminals we do not distinguish religion, race, country, or marital status, much less sexual taste, or gender, what we distinguish only classes of criminals by their positions and level of evil. In this sense I say that criminals can seem like a very normal person, the criminal is in a part of our brain and seeks to carry out this criminal behavior, because something external leads it to that, because I am convinced that we are rational beings and we can think what we do, when we lose our reason is when we run the risk of performing an undesirable behavior. However, there are criminals that generate rejection, they are the ones that harm the physical and mental integrity of another person. There are very well-educated and high-class criminals, however, all are summed up in the mire and social degeneration, when they harm others in a general way (damage to society) or in particular (harm to the person).

In the experience of community work, hijacked trucks from the Mexican Navy and army have been found, as well as criminals dressed as soldiers and sailors. We find soldiers working with the Templars. And vice versa. I had to see soldiers with a mustache, earring and tattoos on their necks, which leads me to suspect their involvement in crime and the military.

The Aquila community members dispersed to other guards and others went away from the problem to Colima, Jalisco, United States. We have to meet to finish the initial work and no longer take care of anyone, my colleagues in criminal proceedings told me that our colleagues liberated the town and the neighboring community, that the group is consolidated among several municipalities, so they are gradually gaining ground exaggerated. Our group of prisoners continues to be detained in the prison and that is where I am sharing this book with you.

I'm probably going to get the job of supervisor or general commander because my colleagues have not shown good leadership skills as a command in the community police. Therefore, the tasks of strategy and attacks have to be careful. A mistake costs lives and I don't want more deaths on my side. I want the death of criminals and not of innocents.

Kidnapping of guilty and innocent. Before an arrest, the first thing that appears is the usufruct of the riot and everyone sees in the detainee, obtaining benefits, we start with the captors, they confiscate, steal and extort the victims, they ask for money in exchange for not filing charges and , if the business is confirmed, the detainee is released, as long as he collects the required amount. Otherwise, it goes to process and goes to the next stage of 48 hours before the common or federal Public Ministry, the matter becomes more difficult, therefore, another wool is required or pay the most expensive legal defense, which in the same way it means money, you try luck. If the agent of the public ministry is corrupt, he will accept the business and the detainee is released within 48 hours, otherwise he is honest or does not take risks, the court stage continues.

The court appears in the same way in the MP, the public defender's office, this only gives their signature and does not assist the detainee. They do so in the event of a monetary offer or a monetary impulse from relatives or from the unfortunate or detainee himself, a good amount of money is offered to the judge and he grants the defendant acquittal, otherwise the process must be winnowed for at least two to four years; If the detainee deserved a custodial sentence of 2 and a half years, the defendant has already served it, the judge says that the sentence is 2 years and 8 months, with 3 days so that the defendant does not feel bad, but in the In the case of federal crimes, the indirect amparo lasts up to 2 years. To this we add the four in the process, there are already 6 and many times they are acquitted, not because he is innocent, but because he served more than the time that he should have spent to sentence him, or the sentence was less than the time he served in pretrial detention or paying the penalty.

The injustice system.

The justice system is outrageous, unfortunately it is like that and changing it is a matter of a social revolution, the system changes due to its trajectory and social practice, in minimal appearance, it does not change its essence, but secondary issues and, above all, in its final form to administer justice. There are judges and magistrates who do their job, but the predominant common one is corruption, violation of the process, slowness and mediocrity. This is how a kidnapping of the detainee appears, the repressive apparatus always gains power over the unfortunate prisoner. We are already in prison, we have dirty businesses, without taking into account legal businesses, such as the store and services, we have the sale of drugs, for which a minimum fee must be paid to the prison, to a member of the prison . Another business is the payment of fees for working inside the prison or for receiving or having many common prisons, they seem to be a market, there is everything. Of all the drugs and weapons of different types move. Large amounts of money, as well as the jailers are also involved in the sale of protection and favors, we do not rule out the managers who declare themselves the owners of the place and collect their respective cut for illegal activities within the prison.

Demands make the market, need seeks a solution and many solve their needs by committing illegal acts, within what is illegal is negotiating life, security as merchandise, the wealthy are the agents of the market.

Here in this federal prison money is not allowed, but the economic factor in money and barter does move, the prison has a store where you can stock up on deodorant, paper, cookies, pens, stamps and envelopes for letters, no However, drugs, cell phones and services are sold. Drugs inside the prison cost up to $3,000.00 MXN for a dose of cocaine and the pills have various price variations, a cell phone costs up to 100,000 thousand MXN pesos.

How are they passed? They are passed on by employees or family members, the same drug. Who delivers the money? The money is paid outside the prison in deposits or cash, that is, the relatives are guilty or the friends who are willing to do this. Defenders and prison authorities are often involved. The services are sold the same and it is commonly that of legal advice in the interior, people who know the stages of the process and the resources, as well as know how to promote, I am not wondering about other services, because there are. In common prisons, the only thing missing is the freedom to leave when you want, although many inmates go out to kill or commit crimes with authorization and use hiding prisons.

People in power are spiteful and vengeful, that is proven by evidence. When a person shows them, they retaliate and punish the population, for example, you make an actuary see an error and he, for the next notification, retaliates in time or information; to the judge, it is not possible to differ from his work because then it affects the interested party, here in prison the criminals were knocking on the door to present the laundry service and they took revenge by not giving them access to the shower or bathroom for days; With reference to the high command, we have already pointed out that the people who promote appeals against the acts of the prison command, these take revenge with severe punishments and obstructing access to the judges, everything is promoted through the mail, I I am referring to the procedural impulse, we find ourselves in the prisoner's trap, he keeps the letters until the procedural stage passes and, therefore, the inmate loses the process and appeal promoted. And the winner is the prison, the Government at all levels is vengeful, when someone does something that is not in accordance with the dictator's policies, he takes revenge in any way, so we have: traffic tickets, denial of services, police harassment , rejection of projects. And depending on the severity, even life is taken from the person or community; this is similar in companies, unions, institutions and churches. Revenge is the way to fix the problems of the powerful, of criminal organizations; It is unnecessary to point out so many examples, we already know who is the worst revenge and often without reason, the family.

Criminal organizations apply the worst revenge. Argüendes are crimes that criminals use, that is, gossip can kill people, criminals are the most treacherous and argüenderos, they are worse than magpies and then they get scared or angry with the argüenderos. They apply the yo yes tu no, in prison many güilas or errands circulate, as primary school girls do and also the "panochones" balls get together to share their progress. The culture of hypocrisy and double standards because in front of a person they are one and behind their backs they betray.

Here in prison we share with people who have no way of acquiring the basics, therefore, those of us who have a store give them free stamps, shampoo, notebook, pen and other things, the bad thing is that later those people say that the kind person is stupid for give away, rather than sell the items; The person in need enters into an Express purchase-sale contract with the owner of the thing for sale and the buyer pays with desserts, stamps or postage stamps, at the internal market price for five desserts, these are chocolates, bread, cookies, mammoth, etc. .

The foregoing refers to the activity in federal centers, in common centers if money is handled. Therefore, the commercial flow is vast and the objects are cheaper and more varied. The degree of difficulty to obtain or pass them influences, this determines the price, since this is not determined by natural factors, which determine the price of merchandise abroad.

The spirit of an artist arises in prison when a virtue is found, it develops it and with it it survives, for example, drawing, painting, singing, poetry, writing, composition, music, crafts, etc. The paintings or images of the Virgin Mary are common among the craft repertoire. We have belts, bags, bracelets, covers, smooth saddles, sandals, and so on. This is how they occupy material and disappear pillowcases, socks and sheets. They unravel, cut and make balls of thread to paint, although in more organized prisons they teach painting, drawing, crafts and other trades. And they provide frames, oil paint, special paper, brushes, pencils, feathers and necessary material.

The readaptation is not achieved with a despotic and counterproductive attitude of the guards and staff of the center. The director thinks he is king, the commander feels he is general. The director behaves like a dictator and they see the prisoner as an animal. The master makes a reluctant, negative attitude in the captive against the rehabilitation project. Denying improvement in the criminal is sinking him into the mire in which he lives; many centers deny reading, deny sports, deny making academic advances.

Our defenders are men and women who advocate for us, in Mexico City they have attended the marches, mostly women, they lent them a house, in which they attend, where our compañeras, wives, cousins, compañeros stay. and relatives of political prisoners; They manifest themselves in our favor, so that the Government recognizes our innocence, however, it has not recognized, despite the fact that the attorney gave a period of 20 days to resolve or give an answer.

Our hope is firm, we hope to leave in the next 3 months of 2014. It is said that the leader of the comments came to speak with the attorney, I do not know the agreements they have entered into.

Day 126, the 33rd birthday.

Today was a special day in my life. I have reached the age when Don José Ramírez Verduzco became a martyr for his people. And that is the age when Christ was sacrificed for the sins of his people. It is my age when I find myself in prison, accused of fictitious crimes invented by criminals. They are the ones to blame for the deaths of their fallen comrades, they are from organized crime, they are the ones who have become filled with greed and arrogance. They don't mind killing innocent people. And they strengthen those who have killed many people, just for feeling that they are the owners and lords of the territory, of the lives of others and all our heritage.

I couldn't communicate with my family because the staff at the center don't do their job and because there is a monopoly in the Community, in the telephone company, they have entered into a contract only with Telmex and I don't know if the line to the house belongs to another company, that is that our relatives have to buy a Telmex telephone line to be able to receive our calls, since the law prohibits monopolies, but here in the prison no law applies. Only the king of this small country, whose name is the director, and his country is the eastern prison number 5, is in charge. The person in charge of the telephone area said that the security department does not do its job and I see that neither the technical area nor social work no area, all are omitted and mediocre. The life of a prisoner is not dealt with under criminal proceedings, but rather at the will of the capricious disabled personnel who work in the prison, who work here because they do not deserve another job.

Today I feel powerless to get up and exercise, or talk to criminals. I hear them talk and they make me lazy, I hear them praise God at the top of their voices, they weaken me and make me ashamed because I know it's pure farce. They don't do it from the heart. That's why my desire overwhelms me, and listening to them is a sacrifice, the prison guard becomes more despot and punishing every day, they have denied us the opportunity to go out to the patio to play for a week.

Day 127.

Friday December 20. Using force we managed to get them to take us out to the patio, but they don't lend us balls to play with, we apply force to things, we hit the doors until they give a solution to the request, but today we didn't do the same, we better opt for sleep or do what everyone wants to do in their room or cell.

I have the pending birth of my son, I feel sorry for my wife, I don't know who will help her, poor and with a new son, I hope to get out of this soon to help my family, I want to meet that gentleman who is going to be born in the next few days, to my son José Emiliano. I want to give him lots of hugs, my wife tells me that he looks very handsome, healthy and with a split piocha. I hope to be free soon. I have missed many things by being here, he said. I want to go into the world and no longer let go of many things that I can do, including loving my family very intensely. And to the people who love me. I want to see the stars, admire the moon, the sun, breathe the scent of flowers and kiss the lips of a rose. Work hard for my children and finish my degree that the government truncated me, and in the same way I long to find a perfect place for my old age, a ranch with many trees and water, I will look for the best place to plant. The end of my life among animals and plants, next to my children and grandchildren, I know that nothing is certain. Just as yesterday I was in full freedom, today I can die or continue in prison with more censorship; I only ask to see my daughter again and meet my son, that would comfort me a little, although my desire is to grow old next to my children and wife.

This 12/28/2013 there is the possibility of knowing about my family, although I prefer that they help my wife in her delivery. I hope in God that he softens the hearts of judges and accusers. The crimes that we bring are few, of course, compared to criminals who bring up to 15 kidnappings, homicides, robberies, etc. Ours is a matter of politics.

Today they took me out to the maximum security patio area for 30 minutes, they took us out to the humiliating 3 by 3 fence. A cube in which they lock us up to get sun. It is a nuisance because it is the place for those punished and for highly dangerous criminals. Already being locked up, everyone in their box sees the director of the prison coming. He told me: "Good morning!" I remained silent for a few seconds because pride and anger did not let me answer. "Don't you know how to answer?" He asks in a threatening tone. I approached him and said: "How is it going to be a good day for me in this place of punishment? If I'm not punished and the punished are playing there on the courts. I am not punished." He replied: "We are going to alternate the spaces." Like wanting to convince or comfort me. "Okay, sir." I told him as if to send him to hell, he went greeting the other inmates, repeating what he said to me in the form of consolation, I know that it is very risky on my part to take an attitude contrary to the disposition and mandate of these security bureaucrats , but courage and anger blinds people, at least me. Retaliation may be taken against me. I don't care, they treat me like a truly dangerous person and I experience all those punished and suffering just like any criminal.

Being undisciplined is the fault of the institution, because it mixes sentenced people with defendants and, even worse, it brings together low profiles with dangerous ones. The work of the institution is lousy, they do not do professional, serious work and they want to readapt the inmates with inhumane measures. It is a shame that the prison system; It makes me angry that the director appears when they take us out as if mocking, one of the explanations given by the inmates of the room I am in, is that those on the second and third level had a mini riot or stopped receiving food for 2 meals and They blamed the level I'm at for devising the action. Be that as it may, I have not participated in these insignificant actions and my claim is for the undignified treatment they give me, I did not swallow the desire to tell the director that I receive something that I do not deserve, and that is injustice.

Hypocrisy is used by the Government to evade any opinion. When human rights visitors attend. They sweep the patios very well and wash corridors, when there is a visitor on the way to the prison, they take us out to play sports and the director, very kind, greets the inmates as if it were a good relationship between inmates and managers. However, it is fallacious and merely a hypocritical expedient. Used by the elite to impress the guest, their hierarchical superior. As an example we have the distribution of clothes in the Porfiriato, due to international visitors. The people sold the rags to have enough to eat for a day. In the towns they hang strings, sweep the streets and water them, when it comes to the visit of a public official, this so that the ruler gets a good impression.

For 15 days the treatment for those of us in the rows has been harsh and worse punishment. They have denied us the bathroom and for 2 days and they take us out to bathe in the morning, with ice water, it feels like it burns, like cuts; Well, the temperature drops to -6 degrees Celsius on this mountain. The cold is deadly, however, some of the inmates comment that before they were doused with ice water and left in the punishment area, where I had the meeting with the director.

The 130th day of my cloister.

For an hour they kept them in punishment, wet and very cold, that is a clear example of torture and it is not possible to tell the human rights visitor, with evidence, the damage received, nor is it possible to go to the judge and prove the damage caused.

These are not social readaptation centers, that's a lie. They are business centers, crime generation. I hope soon to get out of this baseness in which they keep me. God knows that I find myself unjustly imprisoned, that those who owe it walk free among the rulers. My belly burns with anger from all this, but it's just impotence and anger.

I dreamed that a cat took my breath away, a gray cat, behind my ear it obstructed my breathing and I complained, it was because I have a bad nose, it gets congested from the cold and the deviation in my septum causes nightmares, when I reacted I wanted to hit the cat, but it escaped.

In the profiles of the criminals we find a constant, the criminal never exceeds that profile, if he commits a homicide with the chances of winning and his will remains with them forever, in the homicide committed at an early age, the criminals do not mature their personality. They are entirely immature, although they appear authoritative and reasonable, they end up committing more crimes and never get over their way.

Here in the prison I have known several criminals for homicide, one of those homicides was committed inside the walls. He has committed homicides for the proven crime. Out there they gave him 30 years, he entered at 20, he already served his sentence, but they found another intramural homicide and they gave him 15 more. It will come out of almost 70 years. He does not have a home, he has no patrimony to support his needs. Nobody waits for you. He has nothing to live for and no one to live for. That is why he commits and will commit more crimes, he expects him to live in prison until his death or go out to commit crimes. Under this inertia of criminal behavior and in the conditions of the prison system, it is difficult to achieve social rehabilitation because everything is against it. The system hooks and marks forever, like criminal records deny employment and the government allows it. There is constant harassment of justice, society points out and rejects those who have a criminal record. Those attached to the penitentiary system are fired upon release with the phrase "here we are waiting for you". Many live doped, they do not get used to life in prison, but they no longer see a better way to live.

It is like that worthy of times of slavery who had the bad luck of falling into the hands of a slave owner and with blows they break his honor, pride and dignity. In our current system, many free are modern slaves. There are criminals whose illegal status is due to need and conditions of lack, there are those who are imprisoned for an object of 100 MXN, for not having to pay their bail, these people could be productive in some trade, it is only a matter of channeling their energies and their poverty. It is due to the social system in which we live. Criminals like ministerials who perform their role as hit men and mercenaries, those who shoot them; there is another profile of criminals, those who make their way of life a constant transgression of the law and those who administer justice, are another type of criminal. Many times they play the role of judge, party and employer or boss, it is when the crime reaches the controls and elements in which we trust.

Many criminals are imprisoned for less than the innocent, by itself, the system is unfair, obsolete, corrupt, slow and bureaucratic. Those of us below will not have justice until we really want to end this plague. They are as abundant as cockroaches, some already look like turtles because of the shell they carry, there should be no place for criminals other than in jail and in the grave; there is no place for kidnappers, extortionists, murderers, rapists and traitors to the country and others; Anyone who affects the rights of the people must be killed immediately, as well as public and military servants and security forces who commit illegal acts that, due to their seriousness, must die. Indigenous peoples must govern their territory, with full control of their land and laws. They must form their communal guard, their community police, their municipal council of transparency and legality, they must have a jail, a house or a communal palace.

I stopped writing for a few days, the library lent me some books that I had the opportunity to read, I want to justify myself for having some extreme ideas against criminals, first of all, I want to tell you that I am not guilty of the crimes that They are charged for what has generated a devilish anger and I would like justice to be like a work of art, that it be built to perfection and that the culprits could be discovered and that the penalties be paid according to the wickedness applied in the conduct, notwithstanding judges are humans who are often wrong. There are excellent judges whose work is carried out in accordance with the law, but there are factors that influence such as an unscrupulous defense or an excellent defense.

In the month of January 4, my son José Emiliano was born, a baby with blue eyes and white color, I long to meet him and I would give a lot to have the opportunity to kiss him and hold him in my arms. Today I have a phone call and they have induced labor so that my son is born on this day. There is a problem at the prison telephone booth, the line is failing and in the same way we could not link the call to the telephone of the house where my wife and my son are in the company of my mother and my two sisters, whom I thank for their support. loyal support and unconditional accompaniment in this process.

My sister María Isabel is a very precious woman in all her aspects, an exceptional nurse and an excellent character that allows her to be the best nurse in Colima, every day she prepares to be a better professional, she has had her own initiative to improve and professionalization of her career, with her we have shared shortcomings, difficulties, absences and many other wonderful things that make life beautiful. My family is living in a house that my sister has lent us and I feel very grateful to her. My sister María de Jesús is studying her master's degree at the Nicolaita University in Morelia, she has similarly suffered deficiencies, which, although they have not stopped her path to continue studying, have caused her difficulties.

My mother is a humble woman who has raised her children honestly, with dignity and a lot of effort, she was widowed at 37 and no longer sought a love relationship, apart from the fact that the death of my father hurt her a lot and she mourned him, dressed in black, for many years. I still remember their thorny skin from the huisaches, their heels split due to the dryness generated by the dust and the adverse factors of working in the fields. She walked carrying the machete on her shoulder with her heart withered by the pain left by the absence of her lover, that sad woman, but with dignity and honor, sometimes carrying a 45 caliber squad in her bag and with the conviction of carrying the ideal of his family to move forward. My mother with a tough but kind character, whenever she has been asked and has had help from people who are often ungrateful.

Today was an excellent day to play soccer, I played with "el Paquito" a plaza boss of the zetas, there is also "El paisa", a boss of a clique or gang of cholos called "los paisas", there is also "el Teo" an old zeta who is very generous and claims to be a great paid executioner, on the other hand there is "el chilango" a crazy, dangerous guy but he has stated that he is good to his server, I do not forget "El Wili" a zeta who He extorted money from his family, border businessmen, but this voucher did not like to work, like many; In the same way we have "la flor" a doctor from the Michoacán family, he fell for going to visit his brother in Michoacán and while visiting, the government imprisoned him for finding bodies at the time of his arrest.

We have another fine person "el pepe" a young countryman from Michoacán who was notified that his sister was dismembered in Los Reyes Michoacán, he brought organized crime fights as opposed groups between his father and his uncle, the uncle murdered his own brother, that is, the father of "el pepe"; we also have the companion of "la barby" a good firewood guy; In short, we found approximately 20 inmates with the intention of playing a soccer game, we started walking around the perimeter of the field, while your server was approached by different unfortunates and they asked me if I could promote service protections for different acts of violation. , others ask me what to do in their case, in short they invade my space.

We decided to play soccer, a very good game, very dangerous, but we have a non-aggression pact and no fights between us. "El Paquito" fell and dislocated a finger, I had to see the panicked face of this voucher, I could not believe that so many evils he did to society and he was panicking (scared) with a dislocated finger. In that place it is cold all the time, that is why we had to keep moving, walking and doing physical activity. The first thing that is done when entering a field is to check if there are "wilas", that is, messages wrapped in plastic and thrown tied to a stone, then what proceeds is to send it to the addressee, that is the internal mail.

Method to upload the "wilas" to its addressee from the coolers, the building has three floors, the ground floor are the coolers, the second and third floors are for punished; A thread made of a sock is lowered from the upper part and a tube of toothpaste is attached to the end. "The wila" is tied and the messengers deliver the message in exchange for some dessert.

In this place are the leaders of the cartels and the most dangerous, it is the place where they have sent me from the beginning, "the coolers." One of the inmates has introduced approximately 20 doses of drugs to celebrate his birthday, each inmate has been ordered to give a dose, the one with the voice gave his respective dose, the monetary value is three thousand pesos. For that contraband, the inmate paid a high amount of money, but it was the way to celebrate his birthday.

During the visit to the hospital I found my countryman "pepe" under controlled medication, he lost track of himself, it was the last time I saw him, "la flor" was given pills to control his mental problems and he collected them to raise his dose when he put together aXCas six or more, he took them together and he got really lost, he broke his nose and he didn't even understand it. This doctor had his life destroyed, he had a residence in the United States and an excellent job in a hospital in Los Angeles and having a very organized family changed his destiny.

Several of the residents of this area remained during my instance, that leads him to know the cases of each one, some expose their misdeeds with great pride, for counting how many victims they dissolved in acid and how their limbs were dismembered. If you could record your conversations and be able to contribute them to your criminal case, it would be of great help to the judge in making a decision.

Heading for freedom.

A colleague has come to my cell, a room for one person, I talked with him for a few hours, it will be a very uncomfortable room because the space of 1.70 meters by 2 meters is a very small space for two, I think I'm going to spend it very badly. After three hours they announce "Magallón" I gather my belongings, after about two minutes, I already have my package ready to move, they take me to another module, also the coolers, but for two residents, I had to share a room with "the Uncle" Cesar Iván from Veracruz, a merchandise smuggler from the port of Veracruz, a very good person, except that he had to be thrown a ball and paid for the crimes of his boss, the uncle was about 55 years old and his mother, a woman, visited him kind old lady The punishment decreased with the company, since my partner was a guy with an acceptable cultural level. He told me that he had won a chess tournament and we began to make a board with his pieces. We make the board on notebook cover paper, the pieces of tortilla mace with soap, toothpaste and other ingredients. I played him the first game and I beat him, he got upset and we played the second game and I beat him again and we played the third game and we were tied, he didn't want to play me anymore. We opted to play other games.

The uncle was very obese and we agreed to exercise and that's how it was, we started with routines for half an hour, then we managed more time, the uncle began to lose weight, we decreased the tortillas and also the sadness, my friend managed to lose approximately 30 kilos in the time we were in company.

My daughter came to see me and I felt very happy, I wanted to eat her with kisses but my daughter didn't call me dad, she told me uncle, it turns out that my brother José made a pact with her, he told her that as long as her father was not there he would be her father and that once her father returned the game would end, my brother did this because my daughter lasted three days without eating due to the absence of her father and the trauma she suffered when hearing those bullets that stunned her little ears, because as I commented, at the crossing of the Aquila river, they made them cross the river with bullets. Later, my sister Isabel went in a taxi from Colima for my daughter dressed as a nurse and took my daughter, the checkpoint was very aggressive with the civilians and my sister was only asked if the girl was hers and my sister said yes. My wife went in a truck full of women after the community prisoners, later they suffered an attack, because they burned their truck, thanks to a federal patrol the criminals did not conclude with the attack, some trucks full of scourges sought to kill the women .

Being in the room for two the anxiety decreased and from there I could yell out the window at my classmates, I asked them to sing me a song and they had a group "los destrampados", they played with objects and sang good songs that, due to the lack of they enjoyed themselves a lot. I asked them many times for "the black stockings", "thirty cards", "even if they throw their claws at me", etc.

I could send them "wilas" with messages, I had some pictures made with pens, among the favorites was a caricature of an Atlas fox for my son José Emiliano, these pictures were made by the son of Jesús Octavio Jiménez, a crazy friend who was the head of the Armed arm of May, I well remember that he did not want to charge me for desserts because I wrote a criminal complaint against his captors who stole diamonds, rubies, a rolex watch with diamonds, a chain with a pendant with diamonds and money, when he They moved from highlands to perote in the inventory their belongings still appeared but their belongings of approximately two million pesos disappeared; Your server promoted various injunctions and complaints against the prison, this generated acceptance from the criminal leaders and they never bothered me.

In those cells there were two wings, one for heterosexual inmates and the other for active and passive, as it turns out that in one of the cells that was in front of the heterosexuals there was a homosexual couple and one of them had seizures and also tested positive for HIV, this sank him emotionally. This guy was in prison for several federal crimes, most likely he would die in prison.

Returning to my fellow community members, of whom I have hardly spoken, we met 40 boys and some older ones, the young peasants and indigenous people changed and painted their skin with ink, they put pearls on their penises, they cut their hair like cholos and changed their attitude. I don't understand if they did it as a form of appearance and hide behind an attitude in front of the other inmates in order not to show weakness, I learned that they physically fought and some went to the punishment area which was in the upper part of the area where the voice was located.

Castillo's lawyers come for us by private plane, by helicopter, they call us and promise us that we will leave in 15 days, they make us sign a document of agreements, the days go by and no release is made, it was said that it was A matter of time, I spoke with my defense lawyer and apparently he did not want to risk being asked for the return of the five million he had charged for releasing us and he suggested that I not sign any paper and that he guaranteed me that I would be released very soon. One afternoon the lawyers from Castillo go again, Castillo was a federal government delegate that they sent to Michoacán to negotiate with the self-defense groups, because the lawyers told me to give them a vote of confidence, to sign the transfer, I thought about the words from my defender, that accepting such a proposal was condemning me to submit to the government's conditions and would betray all the organizations that lent me a hand. My colleagues had already signed and I refused to sign and my colleagues were upset, because we were in a shed, for which I told lawyer Espino, give me the sheet and I signed.

Day 335 in prison.

July 18, 2014 was a morning like any other, very cold in but Veracruz, a jailer told me: "Magallon" you have two minutes to fix your things, I told my cellmate that I was leaving and he gave me a hug He told me to fulfill all my goals and ideals, wish him luck and may God assign us the best, I changed all his new clothes and took his old ones. I gave him store-bought toothpaste, shampoo, doorbells, and other items. I took my bundle of blankets and made myself available to the jailer, he was pressing me and I told him, well today if I agree with him, we shouldn't take long to go for freedom, I hurried and with my heart already breaking out I went with the mattress on the back, all my belongings and among them I carried the emotions that wanted to swallow me with joy. In the corridors I found one of my fellow community members and greeted him: - quiubo compa! And he asked me "are we going out yet?" I replied: – "I think so, compa" and they took us to the prison reception where there were a lot of happy compañeros.

They put us in a small truck that had the seats upside down, so we felt a very strange sensation, in that truck there were only colleagues plus a federal agent and Jesús Octavio, who was apparently drugged, told the guard about things and the guard laughed, told him some jokes, when minutes before that fucking jailer had behaved like real shit, yelling in our ears and calling out shit, smacking and multiple humiliations. The Zambada's compa told him I'm going to kill you and your family, the guard apologized to everyone and told us that they had done wrong, that their bosses forced them to be shit by protocol, he said that we were going out, that we should maintain discipline in front of federal agents.

The truck took us to the airport in Puebla, from there they put us on an old federal government plane, the federal agents hit us on the head, yelled at us, called our shit, forbade us to look at them because of what they forced us to bring Head between knees the entire flight, we arrived in Uruapan and I said goodbye to my friend Zambada, who apparently was taking him to Sinaloa or Guadalajara.

The heat shock was clearly coming from the pole to the equator, it was the most disastrous climatic change that my body has experienced, they put us in a van type trucks and transferred us from Uruapan to Apatzingán, to a jail that instead of a jail looked like a neighborhood neighborhood, we arrived dying of heat, some of us had our jackets on because we were not allowed to remove them because of the handcuffs, we arrived at the reception of the new prison and the director welcomed us, told us that we were at home, that he wanted us to maintain order and soon we would go to our homes.

That day was a special meal, the prison was governed by community members, in that prison they received us with carnitas, after the carnitas they gave us a tour, the leaders introduced themselves and one who seemed more delinquent than community called a meeting and told me They were appointed as the leader of the group in my region within the prison. Later he called me into his office, it was an air-conditioned room, with some bottles of Buchanan's 12, 18 and beer. He told me that in the prison he was in charge and that whatever they wanted he would do, I asked him for a folder of beer for my group and some boxes of cigarettes, in a short time we already had the party, we also ordered medicine for a first cousin who had been suffering due to kidney failure.

After our arrival, at night, the television news broadcast the news that the Aquila community members had been released and it was not true. The next day our families went to visit us, I met my son José Emiliano when he was 6 months old, a man as a baby, with blue eyes, blond hair and blond hair. I tell you that my sister gave me her son before mine and I looked for the resemblance and found features of my brother-in-law, so I told my sister, this baby is not mine, you changed it for me, she laughed and My wife gave me my precious son, I carried him for a long time, we ate together with my mom, my sister, my brother-in-law, my wife, my daughter Jimena, my niece Sara and William, I hugged them all, kissed them and they left However, I asked for conjugal cohabitation for the following week and it was my wife, we spent a passionate night, where our frustrations and bad experience were vented. I thanked God for having met my son and for finding loyalty in my wife.

The days in that prison were volatile, we played betting soccer and there was a volleyball tournament, the cousins of "La Naranja" were hawks to play volleyball, they got turned on when they played and the inmates inside that prison didn't beat them, but They took some girls to them who did beat them and they were right, my cousins lasted the entire time without playing for almost a year, therefore, they did not bring optimal condition or the radical change in climate and altitude they favor. The boys' team, preferably of the same sex, were very effective in their game, however, it should be noted that it was not easy for them to win, the difference was by a few points.

The community meeting and the escape plan, the leader told us we are going to escape, the plan is as follows: at night a couple of riots will come and tear down the gate, we are going to go up quickly and the riots They are going to take us to a remote place where they are waiting for us to protect us from the government. I want to hear from the groups who agree and if they give their vote. All the groups spoke and some said yes, but the groups were small and the largest group was mine and I told them, comrades, the plan is very good and tempting, but my group is not going to escape, if you want to go Good luck, my group will stay and we will wait for the release order that won't be long. Many groups agreed with that of the voice and the proposal was demolished by vote. That same day, but at night the director of the prison told us, around 11 at night, those from Aquila, gather your things and I'll give you half an hour, they're leaving.

I gathered my personal belongings, we got together and decided to give the community inmates all the groceries we had received from our relatives, who sent us many boxes with various things. We give away our beige clothes from the federal prison. Those jackets that did us the favor of growing up when we entered the Apatzingán common law prison in uniform. The minutes passed as if it were an eternity. We lay on the ground waiting for release and nothing. Around three in the morning they opened the door for us and just took us out into the street, they didn't even apologize. They left us vulnerable, in the lion's den. For that, we had already told our relatives to come for us in closed van-type trucks. We waited until around 7 in the morning for the community members to come for us.

They held an assembly in the maneuver yard of the Aquila community enterprise and I found the pseudo-journalist, whom the women made him run up the hill, leaving cameras and a truck lying around, he went all scared up the mountain to where the soldiers were asking for help. , that because they wanted to kidnap him. That day of the liberation I confronted him and told him that he was a mercenary of information and a coward, he nervously hid behind Cemeí Verdía's back, now he was on our side, when in the raising of arms he even shot us with gargles.

Seeing the panorama of that armed struggle, I decided to retire because it no longer convinced me and I chose to give time to my children and grow my family. I learned that after a certain time groups change and become petty, people without ideals become criminals. Although my group had an oath to leave the fight, our fight had already passed. Days later I read a message from the leader where he said: "beware of my cousin Magallón, because he is a traitor, they saw him embraced by the opponents in Zapotán." That gave me courage and I realized that our head had been lost. I chose to walk away. In a way, let others do things.

Years later, the new groups became corrupted and the affiliation of unity between cartels came, they became what they were fighting. Today Michoacán is a mine of criminal cells that have murdered thousands of people, thousands exiled, thousands disappeared, hundreds of denunciations and complaints of human rights violations. A hostile and dangerous territory.

This was my stay of 350 days in prison for opposing extortion and bad practices in my communal territory of the indigenous community of Aquila, Michoacán, while the government made pacts with crime, the people rose up in arms, not However, violence does not always bring peace, it must be in accordance with the need and not stray from the ideals or the end sought. In my experience I can say that bars kill prisoners, but never free men, I mean this in the sense that there are prisoners who walk the world, prisoners of their emotions, passions, vices and pathologies, on the other hand, men free and of good customs they can be hurt, hurt, imprisoned, but they will not touch their ideals because they are universal, unbreakable and, above all, pure. This is only achieved when the environment strengthens you, when your family does not abandon you and is convinced of your innocence, legitimacy and loyalty to your people.

Don't miss out!

Visit the website below and you can sign up to receive emails whenever Juan Manuel Ramírez Magallón publishes a new book. There's no charge and no obligation.

https://books2read.com/r/B-A-AFPZ-UWVMC

BOOKS 2 READ

Connecting independent readers to independent writers.

About the Author

Juan Manuel Ramírez Magallón
	Filósofo y abogado escritor independiente de Michoacán México